FULL FRONTAL FEMINISM

JESSICA VALENTI

FULL FRONTAL Feminism

A YOUNG WOMAN'S GUIDE TO WHY FEMINISM MATTERS

SEAL PRESS

Full Frontal Feminism
A Young Woman's Guide to Why Feminism Matters
Second Edition
Copyright © 2007, 2014 by Jessica Valenti

Published by
Seal Press
A member of the Perseus Books Group
1700 Fourth Street
Berkeley, CA 94710

ISBN-13: 978-1-58005-561-1

Library of Congress Cataloging-in-Publication Data

Valenti, Jessica.
Full frontal feminism : a young woman's guide to why feminism matters
/ Jessica Valenti.
p. cm.
Includes bibliographical references.
ISBN-13: 978-1-58005-201-6
ISBN-10: 1-58005-201-0
1. Feminism. 2. Women—Social conditions—21st century. I. Title.

HQ1155.V35 2007
305.42—dc22

2006038573

10 9 8 7 6 5 4 3 2 1

Cover design by Faceout Studio, Emily Weigel
Interior design by Megan Cooney

To Miss Magoo

Contents

NEW INTRODUCTION 1

1 YOU'RE A HARDCORE FEMINIST. I SWEAR. 5

2 FEMINISTS DO IT BETTER (AND OTHER SEX TIPS) 19

3 POP CULTURE GONE WILD 43

4 THE BLAME (AND SHAME) GAME 63

5 IF THESE UTERINE WALLS COULD TALK 85

6 MATERIAL WORLD 115

7 MY BIG FAT UNNECESSARY WEDDING AND OTHER DATING DISEASES 135

8 "REAL" WOMEN HAVE BABIES 157

9 I PROMISE I WON'T SAY "HERSTORY" 171

10 BOYS DO CRY 189

11 BEAUTY CULT 203

12 *SEX AND THE CITY* VOTERS, MY ASS 219

13 A QUICK ACADEMIC ASIDE 233

14 GET TO IT 243

RESOURCES 257

New Introduction

When I wrote *Full Frontal Feminism* over five years ago, I couldn't have imagined the response it would get. It's the best-selling book I've written, the one I get the most emails about and the one that seems to have had the most impact. Young women still come up to me and tell me that *FFF* is the book that made them realize they were a feminist. That's a wonderful feeling.

FFF is also a book that's received a lot of criticism—a lot of it fair, some of it not (in my humble opinion!). And while five years is a relatively short amount of time to have passed after writing a book, in feminist years—considering how much has happened in politics, society, and the movement—it feels like forever. That's why I'm so grateful to have the opportunity to republish the book with this new introduction. It gives me the chance to check in with readers, address some of the gaps in the book, and add updates to various issue areas. Because, let's face it, *a lot* has happened!

But first things first: You may have noticed that the cover of the book is different than the original.

We've changed it because the original cover doesn't reflect the kind of feminism I believe in or would like for the world. The original art—featuring a toned white stomach with book's title scrawled across it—centered a particular kind of woman as "feminist" and perpetuated the idea that feminism is largely for white women. At the time, I looked at the cover image and thought of Kathleen Hanna writing the word "SLUT" on her stomach. I thought of it as reclaiming the female body.

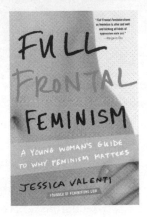

Thanks to the privilege I enjoy as a white person, I could look at that stomach, at the cover, and feel it spoke to me—because *most* images look like me, are relatable, and address who I am because of the culture we live in that centers "white" as "normal." I'm sorry that the book's cover made some women feel that *FFF*—or feminism—wasn't for them. It's a hurt I can't undo, but I'm thankful that future editions of the book will have a new cover.

Another glaring gap in the book was the absence of trans issues and activism. When I wrote the book, trans issues were—for the most part, and wrongly—not seen as an integral part of feminism. Transfeminism was largely absent from women's studies classes, feminist texts, and widely fought feminist issues. Even discussions of intersectionality—fighting racism, classism, and homophobia along with sexism—often didn't include discussions of trans issues. For me, it was reading Julia

Serano's *Whipping Girl*—released the same year as *FFF*—that changed my feminist world. I'm so glad that today—thanks in large part to people like Julia and trans feminists online—trans issues and the discrimination and structural violence against trans people has become such a central part of feminism. There's still much work to be done—by me included—but I believe we're on the right track.

FFF was also criticized for its informal tone and, let's face it, my penchant for dropping the f-bomb and other assorted curses and colloquialisms. I admit, while re-reading the book I cringed a bit at my language—but hey, I'm in my mid-thirties now and have a different perspective than I did in my late twenties. I can understand why a more conversational tone might not be for everyone, but I actually think this was one of the reasons why the book resonated with so many young women. That's how I talked when I wrote the book! One of my hopes for *FFF* was that it would be accessible, that it would feel like listening to a friend. And though I do have a graduate degree in Women's and Gender Studies, I reject the idea that feminism needs to be couched in academic language in order to make it relevant or important. So long live f-bombs!

Probably the most amazing thing that has happened since *FFF* was first published is the absolute explosion of online feminism. When I was writing *FFF*, I was just two years into having founded Feministing.com. More feminist blogs were cropping up every day, but the feminist blogosphere was still a relatively small place. And social media hadn't taken off yet— Twitter had just been founded, Facebook was still a closed network, and Tumblr didn't exist. The rise of these mediums in the last few years has meant that feminism and feminist voices have been amplified in a way we never could have imagined. We've seen President Barack Obama elected (twice!), watched as the "war on women" dominated the media, and seen young feminist activists take the helm online and off.

The rise of insurgent feminist voices combined with a political climate that has become increasingly centered around women's issues has made for a very interesting few years for feminists! For every chapter I wrote, every issue I addressed, there have been setbacks and successes, new thoughts and actions. I've included some (because there's certainly not enough room for all!) at the beginning of each chapter. I'd like to think of these as a bit of a catch-up on individual issues.

Broadly speaking, however, I have to say that the years since *FFF* came out have been some of the most exciting I've experienced as a feminist. My hope and vision for more young women calling themselves feminists has become more of a reality every day. And my fears of a feminist movement controlled by a few elite powerful folks at the heads of mainstream organizations have become more and more quelled as online feminists and individual feminist activists and voices gain more traction in feminist spaces and the mainstream world. While we've suffered setbacks, feminism has come an incredibly long way in a short amount of time. I'm so grateful that I got to be a part of that through blogging and writing, and I'm hopeful that I'll continue to be able to do this work—alongside all of you—for years to come.

This is what
a feminist
looks like

YOU'RE A HARDCORE FEMINIST. I SWEAR.

One of the most incredible things about the last few years is the increase of young women publicly identifying as feminists. Yes, the anti-feminist stereotypes still exist, but with the advent of online feminism, those myths have become much easier to debunk. One of my favorite stories to tell when I speak on college campuses is of a teenage girl who emailed Feministing and told us how she came to become a regular reader. She had done a Google search on Jessica Simpson— she was a fan—and ended up on Feministing because we had written a few posts on how creepy Simpson's dad was (virginity pledges, talking about her breasts, etc). She ended up sticking around because she liked what she saw.

And this is what's amazing about online feminism—ten years ago, if a woman was reading a feminist publication it was because she already identified as a feminist. Now, young people find feminism accidentally or randomly—through online searches and social media—all the time. This doesn't mean that feminism has become accepted by the mainstream, of course. Too many people—public figures and regular folks alike—still don't call themselves feminists even though they have feminist values and believe in feminist issues. But the tide is slowly turning. And the more blogs, tweets, Tumblr posts, and Facebook shares that tell young women that they are, in fact, hardcore feminists, the closer we'll get to creating the change we need to make all women's lives better.

What's the worst possible thing you can call a woman? Don't hold back, now.

You're probably thinking of words like slut, whore, bitch, cunt (I told you not to hold back!), skank.

Okay, now, what are the worst things you can call a guy? Fag, girl, bitch, pussy. I've even heard the term "mangina."

Notice anything? The worst thing you can call a girl is a girl. The worst thing you can call a guy is a girl. Being a woman is the ultimate insult. Now tell me that's not royally fucked up. Recognizing the screwed nature of this little exercise doesn't necessarily make you a feminist. But it should. Most young women know that something is off. And even if we know that some things are sexist, we're certainly not ready to say we're feminists. It's high time we get past the "I'm not a feminist, but . . ." stuff. You know what I'm talking about: "I'm not a feminist or anything, but it is total bullshit that Wal-Mart won't fill my birth control prescription."

Do you think it's fair that a guy will make more money doing the same job as you? Does it piss you off and scare you when you find out about your friends getting raped? Do you ever feel like shit about your body? Do you ever feel like something is wrong with you because you don't fit into this bizarre ideal of what girls are supposed to be like?

Well, my friend, I hate to break it to you, but you're a hardcore feminist. I swear.

Feel-Good Feminism

For some reason, feminism is seen as super anti: anti-men, anti sex, anti sexism, anti everything. And while some of those antis aren't bad things, it's not exactly exciting to get involved in something that's seen as so consistently negative.

The good news is, feminism isn't all about antis. It's progressive and—as cheesy as this sounds—it's about making your life better. As different as we all are, there's one thing most young women have in common: We're all brought up to feel like there's something wrong with us. We're too fat. We're dumb. We're too smart. We're not ladylike enough—*stop cursing, chewing with your mouth open, speaking your mind.* We're too slutty. We're not slutty enough.

Fuck that.

You're not too fat. You're not too loud. You're not too smart. You're not unladylike. *There is nothing wrong with you.*

7

I know it sounds simple, but it took me a long time to understand this. And once I did, damn, did it feel good. Why go through your life believing you're not good enough and that you have to change?

Feminism not only allows you to see through the bullshit that would make you think there's something wrong with you, but also offers ways to make you feel good about yourself and to have self-respect without utilizing any mom-popular sayings, like "Keep your legs together," or boy-popular screamings, like "Show me your tits!"

Really, imagine how nice it would be to realize that all the stuff you've been taught that makes you feel crappy just isn't true. It's like self-help times one hundred.

But all that said, I really do understand the hesitancy surrounding the f-word. My own experience with the exercise that kicked off this chapter—"What's the worst possible thing you can call a woman?"—was presented by a professor on the first day of a women's literature class after she asked how many of us were feminists. Not one person raised a hand. Not even me. My excuse-ridden thinking was, *Oh, there's so many kinds of feminism, how can I say I know what they're all about? Blah, blah, blah, I'm a humanist, blah, blah, blah.* Bullshit. When I think back on it, I knew I was a feminist. I was just too freaked out to be the only one raising her hand.

Most young women *are* feminists, but we're too afraid to say it—or even to recognize it. And why not? Feminists are supposed to be ugly. And fat. And hairy! Is it fucked up that people are so concerned about dumb, superficial stuff like this? Of course. Is there anything wrong with being ugly, fat, or hairy? Of course not. But let's be honest: No one wants to be associated with something that is seen as uncool and unattractive. But the thing is, feminists are pretty cool (and attractive!) women.

So let's just get all the bullshit stereotypes and excuses out of the way.

But Feminists Are Ugly!

Yawn. Honestly, this is the most tired stereotype ever. But it's supersmart in its own way. Think about it, ladies. What's the one thing that will undoubtedly make you feel like shit? Someone calling you ugly.

Back in fifth grade, the love of my life was Douglas MacIntyre, who told me I'd be pretty if only I didn't have such a big, ugly nose. I shit you not when I say that for months, every day after school I would stand in front of the three-way mirror in my bathroom, staring at the offending body part and trying to figure out how a nose could go so horribly, horribly wrong.

Ugly stays with you. It's powerful, and that's why the stereotype is so perfect. The easiest way to keep women—especially young women—away from feminism is to threaten them with the ugly stick. It's also the easiest way to dismiss someone and her opinions. ("Oh, don't listen to her—she's just pissed 'cause she's ugly.")

Seems stupid, right? I mean, really, what's with this *na-na-na-boo-boo* kind of argument? Have you ever heard of a Republican saying, "Oh, don't be a Democrat; they're all ugly"? Of course not, because that would be ridiculous. But for some reason, ridiculous is commonplace when it comes to the f-word.

For example, conservative radio host Rush Limbaugh says that feminism was established "to allow unattractive women easier access to the mainstream of society." Okay—have you ever *seen* Rush Limbaugh? Yeah, enough said. Oh, and by the way—I think I'm pretty hot now. So screw you, Douglas MacIntyre.

But Things Are Fine the Way They Are!

What do I know? Maybe things are fine for you. Maybe you're lucky and superprivileged and you wake up in the morning to birds chirping and breakfast in bed and all that good stuff. But chances are, that's not the case.

There are plenty of folks who argue that feminism has achieved its goal. The 1998 *Time* magazine article "Is Feminism Dead?" said, "If the women's movement were still useful, it would have something to say; it's dead because it has won."[1]

There's no doubt that women have made progress, but just because we get to vote and have the "right" to work doesn't mean things are peachy keen. Anyone who thinks women have "won," that all is well and good now, should ask why the president of Harvard can say that maybe women are naturally worse at math and then have people actually take him seriously.[2] Or why a teacher can still get fired for being pregnant and unmarried.[3]

Seriously, are things really cool the way they are when so many of us are puking up our meals and getting raped and beat up and being paid less money than men? And being denied birth control, and being told not to have sex but be sexy, and a hundred other things that make us feel shitty?

Methinks not. It can be better. It has to be.

Feminism Is for Old White Ladies

This one didn't come out of nowhere. The part of the feminist movement that has been most talked about it, most written about, and most paid attention to is the rich-whitey part. For example, back in the '60s and '70s, white middle-class feminists were fighting for the right to work outside the home, despite the fact that plenty of not-so-privileged women were already doing exactly that. Because they had to (more on this later).

Even now, issues of race and class come up in feminism pretty often. But unlike in days of yore, now they're being addressed (not always well, but still). Besides, feminism isn't just about the organizations you see at protests, or what you hear about in the news. Feminist actions—particularly the kind spearheaded by younger women—are as diverse as we are. You'll see what I mean when you get to the end of this chapter: Young women are working their asses off for causes they believe in. Which is why this next stereotype is so annoying.

Feminism Is So Last Week

Every once in a while, there's some big article about feminism being dead—the most famous of which is the aforementioned

Time piece. And if feminism isn't dead, it's equally often accused of being outdated. Or a failure. Or unnecessary.

But if feminism is dead, then why do people have to keep on trying to kill it? Whether it's in the media, politics, or conservative organizations, there's a big trend of trying to convince the world that feminism is long gone.

The argument is either that women don't need feminism anymore, or that those crazy radical feminists don't speak for most women. Never mind that recent polls show that most women support feminist goals, like equal pay for equal work, ending violence against women, childcare, women's healthcare, and getting more women in political office. Here comes that "I'm not a feminist, but . . ." stuff again!

The obsession with feminism's demise is laughable. And if the powers that be can't convince you that it's dead, that's when the blame game starts. Feminism is the media's favorite punching bag.

The horrors that feminism is supposedly responsible for range from silly contradictions to plainly ludicrous examples. In recent articles, feminism has been blamed for promoting promiscuity;[4] promoting man-hating; the torture at Abu Ghraib; ruining "the family"; the feminization of men; the "failures" of Amnesty International; and even unfairness to Michael Jackson.[5] I'm not kidding. You name it, feminism is the cause.

My all-time favorite accusation: Feminism is responsible for an increase in the number of women criminals. You're going to love this. Wendy Wright of Concerned Women for America—a conservative anti-feminist organization—is quoted in a 2005 article, "Rising Crime Among Women Linked to Feminist Agenda," as saying it's pesky feminists who are to blame for the increase of women in prison.[6]

Wright claims that women are committing crimes because feminism has taught them that "women should not be dependent on others" and that "they don't need to be dependent on a husband," which inevitably forces them to "fend for themselves."[7]

Got that, girls? Without a husband to depend on, you'll be a murderer in no time!

For something that is so tired and outdated, feminism certainly seems to be doing a lot of damage, huh?

Obviously there's an awful lot of effort being put into discrediting the f-word—but why all the fuss? If folks didn't see feminism as a threat—and a powerful one—they wouldn't spend so much time putting it down, which is part of what attracted me to feminism in the first place. I wanted to know what all the brouhaha was about.

It's important to remember that all of these stereotypes and scare tactics serve a specific purpose—to keep you away from feminism.

'Cause don't forget—there are a lot of people benefiting from your feeling like shit about yourself. Think about it: If you don't feel fat, you won't buy firming lotions and diet pills and the like. If you don't feel stupid, you might speak out against all the screwy laws that adversely affect women. It pays—literally—to keep women half there. And god forbid you get involved in anything that would make you wonder why in the world women are having surgery to make their vaginas "prettier."[8] (Sorry, I couldn't help but mention it; it's too freaky not to.)

The solution? Don't fall for it. If feminism isn't for you, fine. But find that out for yourself. I'm betting that you're more likely to be into something that encourages you to recognize that you're already pretty badass than something that insists you're a fat, dumb chick.

Femi-wha?

There are so many stereotypes about feminism, and so many different definitions of it, that what feminism actually is gets insanely confusing—even for women who have been working on women's issues for years. But I always was a fan of the dictionary definition. And I promise this is the only time I'll be quoting the frigging dictionary:

fem·i·nism

1 Belief in the social, political, and economic equality of the sexes.

2 The movement organized around this belief.[9]

Hmm . . . don't see anything about man-hating in there. Or hairy legs. Obviously, there are tons of different kinds of feminism and schools of thought, but I'd say the above is enough to get you started. Besides, at the end of the day, feminism is really something you define for yourself.

Sisterhood, My Ass

No matter how clear-cut (or how complex) feminism can be, not all women are feminists by virtue of having ovaries. And that's just fine by me. I realized this in a big way recently. I was quoted in Rebecca Traister's 2005 Salon .com article entitled "The F-Word,"[10] airing my feelings about the word "feminist"—and I got a little pissy. "Part of me gets so angry at younger women who are nervous about feminism because they're afraid that boys won't like them. . . . Part of me wants to say, 'Yeah, someone's going to call you a lesbian. Someone's going to say you're a fat, ugly dyke. Suck it up.'"[11] My attempt to strongly defend the word "feminism" didn't go over well with a lot of people. One woman actually posted a homophobic rant of a response to Salon.com:

> ✺ I'll call myself a feminist when the fat, mannish dykes who do run around calling themselves "Feminist" very loudly and constantly concede that my decision to groom and dress myself as a twenty-first-century professional woman is every bit as valid a choice as their decision to become stereotypical jailhouse bulldaggers. Ovaries only make you female, they do not make you woman, and I am a woman. In other words, I will call myself a feminist when those mannabees are as proud of and joyful in their womanhood as I am in mine . . . Until then, fuck off and take your hairy legs with you.[12]

Ok then! I didn't need much more than this to realize that feminism isn't for everybody. I never really bought the

"We're all sisters" thing anyway. I've met enough racist, classist, homophobic women to know better. Feminism's power isn't in how many women identify with the cause. I'll take quality over quantity any day.

Quality Women

So who are these elusive feminists? Like I've said—you are, even if you don't know it yet. Though I'm hoping by now you're at least slightly convinced. The smartest, coolest women I know are feminists. And they're everywhere. You don't need to be burning bras (actually, this never happened—total myth) or standing on a picket line to be a feminist. Chances are, you've already done stuff that makes you a feminist. You don't have to be a full-time activist to be an awesome feminist.

The work that young women are doing across the country is pretty goddamn impressive. Do they all consider themselves feminists? Probably not. But a lot of the work they're doing is grounded in feminist values. Just a few examples:

A group of high school girls in Allegheny County, Pennsylvania, organized a "girlcott" of Abercrombie & Fitch when the clothing company came out with a girls' shirt that read: WHO NEEDS BRAINS WHEN YOU HAVE THESE? After the group caused quite a ruckus in the media, A&F pulled the shirt.

Two young women in Brooklyn, Consuelo Ruybal and Oraia Reid, used their own money to start an organization called RightRides after a number of young women were raped in their neighborhood. Women can call the service anytime from midnight to 4 AM on the weekends and get a free ride home. Simple, but damn effective. Their motto is: "Because getting home safe should not be a luxury."

The documentary film *The Education of Shelby Knox* was inspired by a high school student in Lubbock, Texas, who took on her town's school board to fight for comprehensive sex education. Shockingly, the abstinence-only brand they were receiving wasn't quite cutting it.

A group of queer women, tired of seeing the art world bypass great women artists, started *riffRAG* magazine. The magazine features work that slips under the mainstream's radar.

Misty McElroy decided to start Rock 'n' Roll Camp for Girls as part of a class project at Portland State University. She expected about twenty girls to sign up—she ended up getting three hundred. Rock 'n' Roll Camp for Girls teaches young girls to play instruments, deejay, sing, and write songs and ends with a live performance. The camp was so popular in Oregon that there are now rock camps in New York City, Washington, D.C., Nashville, Tennessee, Tucson, Arizona, and various California locations.

This is just a small sampling of the amazing work young women are already doing (and they say we're apathetic!), and it doesn't even touch on all the women's blogs, online and print zines, and community programs that are out there. These women and their work prove that feminism is not only alive and well, but also energized and diverse. Not to mention fun.

You can be a feminist without making it your life's work. It's about finding the cause that works for you, and makes you happy, and doing something about it. (Trust me, getting off your ass can be more fun than you think.) For some women, that means working in women's organizations, fighting against sexist laws. For others, it means volunteering time to teach young girls how to deejay. It doesn't matter what you're doing, so long as you're doing something. Even if it's as simple as speaking up when someone tells a nasty-ass sexist joke.

There's a popular feminist shirt these days that reads: THIS IS WHAT A FEMINIST LOOKS LIKE. Ashley Judd wore one at the 2004 pro-choice March for Women's Lives in Washington, D.C. Margaret Cho wore one on the Spring 2003 cover of *Ms.* magazine. I wear one, too; I love this shirt. Because you never really do know what a feminist looks like. And believe me, we're everywhere.

Fucking
while
feminist

2

FEMINISTS DO IT BETTER
(AND OTHER SEX TIPS)

Ah, sex. How little has changed. Not long after I wrote *FFF*, I published a book called *The Purity Myth: How America's Obsession with Virginity is Hurting Young Women*. It looked at America's cultural and political obsession with young female sexuality and how the fear of said sexuality was being used to push a regressive agenda for women's rights. The book came out after Barack Obama was elected and people said to me—what are you worried about?! Abstinence only education is over, we have a progressive president, no one cares about women's sexuality anymore. Besides, I was told, we live in a hypersexual society! The idea that women are still expected to be virginal is ridiculous. Ha.

In the lead-up to the 2012 presidential election, we saw a young woman, Sandra Fluke, called a slut and a prostitute for daring to say she thinks birth control should be covered by health insurance. Those of us who spend a lot of time online have been called whores and sluts for simply blogging about feminism or sex. We've seen young women commit suicide after being slut-shamed and bullied online and off. Women's sexuality is still roundly mocked, commodified, or seen as evil—and that pervasive cultural belief still impacts politics and culture. Thankfully, we're talking about it more than ever. When Rush Limbaugh attacked Fluke, feminists— and nonfeminists—came to her defense and forced Limbaugh to apologize. Slut-shaming online is being countered by a strong—and pissed!—movement of young feminists not willing to take shit lying down. And on the proactive front, young people online and off are redefining what "sex positive" means to them and fighting for a culture that sees female sexuality as natural, normal, and wonderful.

I'm better in bed than you are. And I have feminism to thank for it.

There's nothing more hackneyed than the notion that feminists hate sex (but I guess if you buy the ugly, man-hating stereotype, hating sex follows). Feminists do it better 'cause we know how to get past all the bullshit.

Women's sexuality is often treated like a commodity, a joke, or a sin. This is especially true for us younger women who end up getting totally screwed up by social influences telling us what "hot" or desirable behavior is. (Generally, it's flashing boobs or faux-lesbian make-out sessions. Never been a fan of either.)

When you're getting abstinence-only education during the day and *Girls Gone Wild* commercials at night, it's not exactly easy to develop a healthy sexuality. You're taught that sex be-fore marriage is bad bad bad, but that if you want to be a spring-break hottie, you'd better start making out for the camera.

While these two messages are seemingly conflicting, they're actually promoting the same idea—that young women can't make their own decisions about sex. Whether it's a teacher telling you not to or a cameraman telling you how to, having sex that's about making yourself happy is a big no-no these days. Shit, you can't even buy vibrators in some states!

To get unscrewed, you really need to take a close look at all the insane things stacked up against women having a good old time in bed. And after marveling at the ridiculousness of things like the sexual double standard and the faux-sexy crap that's forced down your throat, you just learn to say fuck it.

Just (Don't) Do It

Women are taught that we're only supposed to have sex un-der these bizarre arbitrary guidelines: only if you're married; only if it's for procreation; and only with another girl if guys can watch. So unless you're going to do it the way other peo-ple want, just don't.

You're a Dirty Lollipop

Nothing freaks me out/pisses me off more than abstinence-only education. Basically, it's the most naive form of sex education you can get: Sex is bad, don't have it until you're married, con-traception doesn't work. Somehow educators think this will convince kids to not have sex. Compare that to comprehensive sex education that teaches abstinence but also makes sure that teens have medically correct information about contraception, STDs, and the like. It's reality-based sex ed that understands that no matter how many scare tactics you throw at people, they're still going to do what they want.

This isn't to say that I think holding off on sex is bad—abstain all you want, ladies. But if you're holding off, do it because you're waiting to have sex on your own terms. And don't *not* have sex because you think you're worthless if you do—which is exactly what these classes are saying.

As it stands now, the government is spending $178 million a year to tell young women they're big whores if they give it up,[1] and various other untruths. Most (80 frigging percent)[2] abstinence-only education programs give out false information about sex—all of it sexist, most of it bordering on the ridiculous.

The medical misinformation is not just untrue—it's straight-up dangerous. For example, these programs teach not only that condoms don't protect you from pregnancy or STDs and HIV, but that they could cause cancer.[3] (Condom cancer?) After kids are exposed to this bullshit, they are less likely to use contraception—'cause it doesn't work anyway, right? Because of abstinence-only education, we're going to have a generation of sexual dum-dums.

It seems unfathomable, but, somehow, teaching the truth about sex and contraception is just too scary for some folks. Conservatives and right-wing religious groups think that it's going to make us all slutty. I know proponents of the all-holy abstinence agenda bristle at the idea of girls being taught how to put a condom on a penis, even though studies show that real sex ed (you know—the kind that tells the truth)

In 2006, conservatives and religious groups tried to block a vaccine that prevents cervical cancer (which kills 200,000 women worldwide every year) because they were afraid it would make teen girls slutty. Better cancer than sex, apparently.

significantly reduces teenage girls' STD rates. Not to mention comprehensive sex ed actually delays teen sex and ensures kids are making informed decisions. Isn't that more important than being afraid that your kid isn't a virgin?

Apparently, not so much. Schools that get federal funding for abstinence-only sex ed *can't* teach safe-sex practices. You heard right. They can't even talk about it. Because god forbid your kids have safe sex. Much better that they resort to only-a-slut-would-use-a-condom sex. But what's just as disturbing as the bad science behind these programs is the unapologetic sexist crap they're spewing.

One program teaches that women need "financial support," while men need "admiration."[4] Another tells students: "Women gauge their happiness and judge their success on their relationships. Men's happiness and success hinge on their accomplishments."[5] Yeah. I'll just let that one sit for a bit.

Another program tells a faux-fairytale that isn't so much about sex as about how women need to keep their mouths shut. One book used in abstinence curricula, *Choosing the Best*, tells the story of a knight who saves a princess from a dragon (original, I know). When the knight arrives to save her, the princess offers some ideas on how to kill the dragon. Her ideas work, but the knight feels emasculated, so he goes off and marries a village maiden, "only after making sure she knew nothing about nooses or poison."

The curriculum concludes with the moral of the story: "Occasional suggestions and assistance may be all right, but too much of them will lessen a man's confidence or even turn him away from his princess."[6]

Hear that, gals? Shh . . . if you let on that you're smart, your prince on the white horse is likely to run scared!

Abstinence programs are also *huge* fans of making sex the ladies' responsibility. It's up to us to make sure it doesn't happen, because guys just can't help themselves. One program actually advises girls:

❋ Watch what you wear. If you don't aim to please, don't aim to tease. The liberation movement has produced some aggressive girls, and one of the tough challenges for guys who say no will be the questioning of their manliness. And because females generally become aroused less easily, they're in a good position to help young men learn balance in relationships by keeping intimacy in perspective.[7]

The logic is laughable. Seems that girls don't get horny, so it's up to us to make sure that The Sex doesn't happen. And if it does, well, you should have kept your legs closed, you big dummy. But really and truly, the following gem is my fave. It comes from an "educator" speaking at an abstinence conference last year: "Your body is a wrapped lollipop. When you have sex with a man, he unwraps your lollipop and sucks on it. It may feel great at the time, but unfortunately, when he's done with you, all you have left for your next partner is a poorly wrapped, saliva-fouled sucker."[8]

Holy. Shit. Is that clear enough for you? Without your precious "lollipop," you're a piece-of-shit, dirty-ass, already sucked-on candy. Which is supposedly why you have to hold on to your most precious commodity—your virginity.

Our Hymens, Ourselves

I have never really understood what the big deal was about virginity. Really. Mine was lost without a great deal of fanfare to a high school boyfriend whom I dated for several years afterward. I expected to feel different—I didn't. The whole precious-flower-virginity thing always seemed silly to me. So imagine my surprise when I found out that I was just a used-up piece of trash (or candy) without it.

Remember how back in the day, your virginity was a valuable commodity and your "purity" was pretty much what your dad banked on to get a good price for when you got married? You think that's all in the past? Not even close.

One of the most disturbing stories I've ever heard was about Jessica Simpson and her dad, Joe. A gossip mag reported that during a ceremony when Jessica was twelve years old, Joe made her promise to stay a virgin until marriage. Wait, it gets worse. Jessica's dad, who is also her manager, gave her a promise ring and said, "I'm going to tell you how beautiful you are every day . . . and I'm going to be that person until the day you find a man to do that in my place."[9]

If you're like me, you're probably in the fetal position on the floor right now, trying to make that image go away. But this isn't unusual—there are virginity cards, rings, ceremonies, you name it. The one thing they all have in common is that girls' virginity and sexuality don't belong to them.

Not only are virginity pledges sooo creepy and wrong, they're not exactly effective. Recent studies have shown that teens who take virginity pledges are actually more likely to have oral and anal sex.

Their logic is that because it's not intercourse, it's not real sex. Somehow I don't think the folks who made up the whole pledge thing had sodomy in mind. (You would think the idea of good Christian girls taking it in the ass would motivate some change in the whole pledge system, but they're sticking to their guns.)

What kills me is that we're falling for this crap. Women feel so bad about losing their virginity that some of them are actually deluded by the idea that they can become "born again" virgins. Like a self-imposed dry spell. For fuck's sake, there are even women who are getting plastic surgery to get fake hymens put back in! Who the hell wants their hymen back?

And the people who are just shocked—shocked!—that younger women are looking to oversexualized pop culture to define themselves are the very same ones that are shoving virginity down our throats. (Not literally, of course. Ew.) For folks who are trying to tell us we shouldn't define ourselves by our sexuality, they certainly can't get past the whole dick-meets-vagina thing. And really, if you want to attach young women's worth to their virginity, you can't be surprised when they follow suit and attach all their worth to their sexuality. You can't have it both ways.

Getting Carded for Sex

In addition to the fact that it's pretty much never okay for women to have sex (unless you're married and doing it to procreate, of course), there's a special emphasis placed on younger women. We're *really* not supposed to have sex.

The logic is pretty simple: Girls aren't supposed to like sex, especially teenage girls. So if you're having sex, either you're a slut or you're a victim who's being taken advantage of. Neither are particularly attractive options. It's like the virgin-whore complex on crack. The idea that teen girls want to have sex is just too much for some people to handle. Girls are supposed to think sex is icky and make excuses about headaches.

I'll never forget the first time I realized just how nutty people could get over the idea of a teen girl's choosing and wanting to have sex. I was watching *Oprah* a while back, when Dr. Phil (pre–self-help empire) was a regular. He was discussing the "problem" of teenage sex. There was one seventeen-year-old on the show talking about how she and

> The U.S. government is expanding abstinence-only programs to target not just students, but unmarried adults. Soon they'll expect everyone to abstain!

her boyfriend had oral sex. She was superarticulate and smart, and made her position very clear. She said she had been with her boyfriend a long time, and they loved each other but weren't ready for intercourse, and so they had decided to have oral sex instead. Dr. Phil ripped into her like a maniac, saying, "A friend doesn't ask you to go in the bathroom, get on your knees in a urine-splattered tile floor, and stick their penis in your mouth." The girl looked at over at her mom and said, "That's not what happened to me," but she was ignored. Nice, huh? But insults and scare tactics against teen sex are par for the course these days.

One conservative Christian group, Focus on the Family, is so concerned about teens having sex that it came out with a study (a very dubious one at that) concluding that having sex before you're eighteen makes you more likely to be poor and divorced.[10] I suppose I have a life of poverty-stricken solitude to look forward to. And that master's degree I have must be a mistake of some sort. Oh, and just so you have some perspective on this, Focus on the Family also made a public statement that accused the cartoon *SpongeBob SquarePants* of promoting homosexuality to children.

No matter how smart and straight-up you are about wanting to have sex, if you're choosing it, you're making a mistake that could ruin your life, or you're a big whore. Done and done. It's no wonder that so many people would rather think of teen girls as victims unable to wrap their poor little heads around the complexities of sexuality.

The victim role is played out in a lot of ways, but the most blatant are seen in our existing consent laws. If you're under a certain age, you can't consent to sex. Period. Now, I'm not going to say that I think consent laws shouldn't exist—clearly, there are plenty of creepy-ass pedophiles running around. But the way that the laws are implemented—not to mention the implication that young women can't make their own decisions about their sexuality—is seriously flawed.

There's a bill in Missouri, for example, that would require teachers, doctors, and nurses to report kids who are sexually active to a state abuse hotline.[11] That's right—have sex, get reported. The kicker? The law says that the sexually active teen need only be reported if they are unmarried. Ahem. Marriage is the ultimate Get Out of Jail Free card—sometimes literally—for teen sex. In a case in Nebraska in July 2005, charges were brought against a twenty-two-year-old man for having sex with a fourteen-year-old girl.[12] A

> The newest trend in anti-sex weirdness is "purity balls," a prom-like event where girls as young as six pledge their chastity—to their dads! Creepy.

bunch of folks weren't too happy about the charge because the "couple" was married after the girl became pregnant. How does a thirteen-year-old get married, you ask? Oh, her parents just took her over to Kansas, where kids as young as twelve can wed with their parents' consent. Lovely.

Clearly, this case is fucked up in a thousand ways. But what really kills me about this was that a large part of the community in Nebraska was pissed that it had even been brought to court, because the guy had done "the right thing" by marrying her. So if you don't get married you're a rapist, but if you do you're a stand-up guy? In either case, it seems to me the point of all this is to make sure that the girl in question (who has no real say in the matter) stays "pure."

This kind of faux concern about teenage girls and sexual activity has nothing do with keeping girls safe. It's about legislating morality and ensuring that someone—whether it be a parent, husband, or the state—is making decisions for young women. Because god forbid we make them ourselves.

Just Do It (If You're So Inclined)

I was serious about feminism making me better in bed. You can't be good in that department unless you get past the anti-sex nonsense, and feminism allows you to do just that.

Feminism tells you it's okay to make decisions about your sexuality *for yourself*. Because when it comes down to it, what's more powerful and important than being able to do what you want with your body without fear of being shamed or punished?

Feminism teaches responsibility. You can't really enjoy yourself sexually if you don't have all the facts and aren't being safe. While conservative programs are doing their best to make sure that you stay in the dark about contraception, feminists are fighting to make sure that you have access to the information and resources you need to have safe sex.

And perhaps most important, feminism wants you to have fun. Sex isn't just about having babies after all, despite what young women are being taught.

"At Risk," My Ass

In itself, the act of having sex is considered irresponsible by some. These days, calling a teen "sexually active" is code for "troubled" or "at risk" (though if they're a product of abstinence-only education, I wouldn't disagree with the "at risk" part).

But really, what could be more responsible than taking control of your body by making informed decisions about your sexuality? What's really irresponsible is telling young women there's something wrong with having sex. Naturally, just calling yourself responsible doesn't quite cut it. I know it's annoying, but sometimes you have to get off your ass and do something.

TAKE RESPONSIBILITY FOR YOUR HEALTH

* Get thee to a gyno! Get regular checkups—no one wants a sick vagina, after all.

* If you've been subjected to abstinence-only education, get out there and find comprehensive information on sex (and pass it around to your friends!). Planned Parenthood is a great place to start; its website has a ton of information: www.plannedparenthood.com.

* Use protection. If you're having straight sex, use two forms of contraception if you don't want to get preggers. One of them must be condoms. Always. Every time.

TAKE RESPONSIBILITY FOR YOUR PARTNERS

* Love and attraction are curious things, and there aren't many women who don't have at least one partner they regret. But that doesn't mean we can't at least try to choose wisely. I never liked the word "promiscuity," because it's defined as having sex indiscriminately. So have sex with whoever you like, and as many people as you like, but I think we can all afford to be *a bit* discriminating.

* Don't have sex with someone who won't use protection.

❀ Don't have sex with someone who is anti-choice—
they have no respect for your body or your ability
to make decisions for yourself.

❀ Don't have sex with someone who doesn't respect
your physical and emotional boundaries.

❀ Don't have sex with Republicans. (Okay, that one
is just mine.)

TAKE RESPONSIBILITY FOR YOUR CHOICES

❀ There'll be plenty on this later, but it's worth mentioning. As you probably know already, when it
comes to the rights we have over our bodies, shit is
going downhill. There are plenty of young women
who don't have access to contraception and abortion. This is unacceptable. Fight the good fight in
your schools, community, wherever, to make sure
that you have as many choices as possible when it
comes to your reproductive rights.

TAKE RESPONSIBILITY FOR OTHER WOMEN

❀ We're all in this together, ladies—so help your fellow woman out. Whether it's taking a friend to
get birth control, helping someone come out, or
even just not calling other girls nasty names—it
makes a huge difference.

See—now no one can give you shit! On to the fun stuff.

From *The Joy of Sex* to Joyless Sex

Can someone tell me when sex became such a goddamn downer? You would think from the way people talk about it these days that intercourse is a potential epidemic—teen girls running around like junkies trying to get a quick dick-fix.

No doubt, there are serious consequences to sex. But if you're well informed and being responsible, what's the problem? We need to get beyond the politics, the religious guilt trips, and the moral tsk-tsking and start to remember that sex is a good thing. A great thing. Perhaps the best thing ever.

Someone handed me a sticker at a women's rights march once. It said: I FUCK TO COME NOT TO CONCEIVE. I can't find that sticker and I want it back! Because what's been lost in this whirlwind of abstinence-only, married-only, straight-only nonsense is pleasure. I don't know about you, but when I have sex it's because it feels good, not because I'm gearing up to knit some booties.

But there are plenty of people out there—powerful ones—who want you to forget that. Take this nut job, for example: Former Senate candidate Alan Keyes once called homosexuality "selfish hedonism," because gay sex isn't for popping out kids; it's just about feeling good. (The horror!) The fact that someone could outright say that it's a bad thing to have sex because it's fun is beyond ridiculous. Because that's the one thing we all have in common. Whether we're married, single, gay, young, whatever—we all want to have orgasms. Unless you're Alan Keyes, I guess.

That's where feminism comes in. Seriously. Feminism says that you have a right to enjoy yourself. An obligation, even. Young women need to get past the bullshit, scoff at the shame tactics, and get back to the hard work of getting off.

> Note: Yes, I realize that I'm focusing on the physical aspect of sex, rather than the emotional. That's because it's generally the physical part where women are getting fucked-up messages about sex.

Reclaiming Your Number

It's easy to say that sex is a good thing. Living it is the hard part. Women have been taught for so long that having sex—or even just hooking up—means that you're a slut, so it's kind of a hard thing to get over. But if sex is a good thing, then why should we be ashamed that we're having it?

It's time to come out of the "fucking" closet!

Most women are all too familiar with the sexual double standard that says women are big hoochies for having sex but guys are players. And while most of us know it's total bullshit, we still follow the rules somewhat. My first experience with the good-girls-don't double standard came after a hiatus with a high school boyfriend. Though both of us had seen other people during our break from each other, turns out I was the big slut. The explanation by my then-boyfriend was predictable: Men are supposed to be slutty and women need to remain monogamous. It's in our genes, apparently.

If someone tries to pull this argument on you, make sure to call bullshit. The whole men-are-driven-to-spread-their-seed thing is just plain archane. Read Natalie Angier's amazing book *Woman: An Intimate Geography* for the hardcore facts. I promise it's worth it.

Since that long-ago high school drama, the sexual double standard has continued to be one of the most infuriating aspects of sexism for me. I've seen otherwise-great male friends

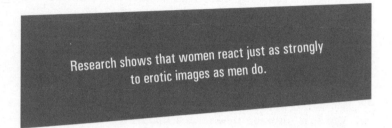

Research shows that women react just as strongly to erotic images as men do.

turn away potential girlfriends because of their number of sexual partners; I've had female friends who, upon hearing my "number," told me I must must *must* keep it a secret. You know, 'cause the more dicks you encounter, the quicker you go to hell.

The Almighty Cock

Rambling aside, why is it that penises define how slutty women are? What about women who aren't straight? According to societal norms, it's not even real sex unless a dick is involved. So should lesbians rest assured that they're not the nasty sluts their hetero sisters are? If I get oral from every girl on the block, am I slutty? (Or just smart?) Sorry, it just makes me crazy that whether I'm a whore is completely dependent on cock.

Cock or not, if it's one person or fifty—why all the shame? If you're making responsible, informed decisions that make you happy, who cares. In the timeless words of Salt 'n Pepa: "If I/wanna take a guy/home with me tonight/it's none of your business."

What's strangest to me is that the same people who adhere to the rules of the double-standard game will admit its flawed logic. Everyone knows it's screwed up; it's just that most people have given up. Or if you're a guy, perhaps you like the idea that you can whore around but "good" girls can't.

So it's really up to young women to fix this mess; we have to take the lead. Young women need to not just ignore the double standard, but to actively fight it by being proud of sex. I'm not saying you should hand out flyers with all the names of your sexual partners and a play-by-play of your favorite positions. But there's a lot of power in just telling the truth without any shame. If you lie about the number of people you have sex with, or if you call another girl a slut and mean it in a nasty way, you're supporting the notion that it's not okay for women to have sex when they want to, or with as many people as they want to. And please note that I'm saying *when* they *want* to. While I know it's all too common, there's nothing lamer than hooking up with someone for reasons other than desire and/or love.

I know it's easier said than done, but there will always be someone who will judge you . . . even if you're not hooking up! I think we all know someone who had a terrible reputation that materialized out of nowhere.

The only way to battle shame is with pride; we have to be proud of the choices we make and stand behind them. We have to take the power out of sexual insults like "whore" and "slut." There aren't many feminists my age who don't remember musician Kathleen Hanna—of Bikini Kill and Le Tigre fame—scrawling SLUT across her stomach as a way to reclaim the word. We need to do the same thing, not just with the word, but with the idea. There's nothing wrong with having sex; don't let anyone forget that.

Beyond Bean-Flicking

I always wondered why there weren't more terms for female masturbation. I mean, men can jerk off, choke the chicken, rub one out, or spank the monkey, but the only one I've heard for women is flicking the bean, and frankly, that just sounds painful. But then I realized that women don't really talk about masturbating all that much, especially younger women. When I was in high school, my friends and I would chat about sexual positions and blow jobs as easily as we discussed our last math class. But masturbation was hush-hush. Looking back, that's just weird. Seems to me that masturbation should be the most-talked-about sex. After all, it is the safest sex of all. (Even emotionally—when was the last time you broke your own heart?) And it's not like most women aren't masturbating. For as long as we've had vaginas, we've been messing around with them—scientists recently found a dildo from the Ice Age.[13] I shit you not.

But unless you're screwing yourself silly in front of a camera for boys' viewing pleasure (you'll see what I mean when you get to Chapter 3, "Pop Culture Gone Wild"), female masturbation is taboo. Probably because it's the ultimate "selfish hedonism." Ain't no way any bean-flicking is going to get you pregnant. Masturbation is just for fun, so it must be bad.

Despite the fact that encouraging young women to masturbate might cut down on STDs, and even lower rates of supposedly evil teen sex, it's really not stressed in sex ed classes. It's just too much for the anti-sex folks to take. In

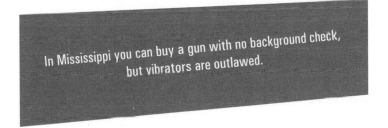

In Mississippi you can buy a gun with no background check, but vibrators are outlawed.

1994, U.S. Surgeon General Joycelyn Elders said that masturbation "is a part of human sexuality, and it's a part of something that perhaps should be taught—perhaps even as part of our sex ed curriculum."[14] Smart lady, right? I thought so, too. Unfortunately, being logical was just as frowned upon then as it is now. She was forced to resign.

But it's not just young women in school who are getting the shaft when it comes to masturbation. Women of all ages are discouraged from taking matters into their own hands. This is not to say that women only masturbate with battery-operated aids, but I think it's telling that pretty much anything that vibrates (and is therefore fun for the ladies) is outlawed in eight states. Seriously—Georgia, Kansas, Louisiana, Mississippi, Texas, Virginia, Alabama, and Colorado all have "anti–erotic massager" laws. Something tells me these states don't have a similar ban on Lubriderm and *Playboy*.

A woman in Texas was even arrested in 2006 for daring to throw a "Passion Party."[15] (Kind of like a Tupperware party, but with naughty stuff.) Arrested! Apparently, in Texas you can sell vibrators, but only if you sell them as "novelties" or "gag gifts." Selling them in a way that admits their actual role in sex is the illegal part. You know, because girls masturbating should be funny, not real. Then, of course, there are the ladies who don't partake because they've internalized the same sentiment that these bullshit laws enforce. This just makes me sad. Did they fall for the vaginas-are-gross thing? Didn't they ever get the hand-mirror lesson?

Please, ladies—if this is you—hop to it! Don't worry, I'm not going to give you any step-by-step instructions; I'll leave that to the sexperts. I will, however, highly encourage some serious self-loving. Shit, it helps you go to sleep; it helps you know your body and be better in bed; it even motivates you to buy fun vibrators that are neon or shaped like rabbits. Oh yeah—and it gives you orgasms. Do you really need any more convincing?

Getting Down to Business

I really couldn't resist writing something about oral sex. Yes, I know it's just one specific sex act and there are tons more, blah, blah, blah. But there is something about oral sex that really has people all riled up lately (especially when it comes to teen sex). Not to mention that sex is so often talked about in terms of penis/vagina intercourse that folks seem to forget that 1. not everyone is straight, and 2. penetration isn't the end-all for women when it comes to sex.

There is also something really interesting to me about the different reactions men have to oral sex. There are the guys who love to give it (treat them well) and can't get enough, guys who will do it as some sort of obligatory rest stop on the way to intercourse, and the guys who are so grossed out by pussy, you have to wonder what went wrong. But what I find particularly interesting about oral is that when it comes to teens and oral sex, it's always shown as girls who are sucking dick left and right with no reciprocation in sight. This myth is used all the time to highlight how girls are being victimized by the supposedly sexually lax attitude in pop culture.

The truth? A September 2005 sex survey of young women showed that the give-and-take when it comes to going down is pretty much equal between guys and girls.[16] So there!

3

POP CULTURE GONE WILD

There's nothing feminists like better than pop culture. Because even when it's bad (and let's face it, for women, it often is VERY bad) we can analyze it! One of the best things to happen in the last five years for feminism is the incredible number of sites dedicated to looking at the relationship between feminism and pop culture, and an examination of popular media and products from a feminist point of view. If you're interested in Disney, there's a Tumblr site solely dedicated to feminism and Disney princesses. If you want think about pop culture from a lens that centers on race, you can check out the amazing Racialicious. In addition to providing a valuable service to feminists and nonfeminists alike, these sites also contribute to the once-dismissed notion that analyzing pop culture is an incredibly important part of feminist activism. After all, how can we get more of *Buffy* or *Scandal* if we're not looking at the ways in which feminism and pop culture intersect?

It's not exactly news that pop culture is all sex all the time. But it's not just "sex"—it's us girls. Pop culture sex is sugar and spice, tits and ass. Sexuality itself seems to be defined as distinctly female in our culture. After all, while billboards and magazine ads may feature a ripped guy from time to time, it's mostly women who make up what sexy is supposed to be.

And it's not just sexy—it's straight-up sex. Pop culture is becoming increasingly "pornified."[1] As pornography becomes more culturally acceptable, and the more we're inundated with sexual messages—most of which are targeted at younger women—the more hardcore these messages become. Yes, I know, sex sells and always has. But do you think that twenty years ago little girls would be taking *Playboy* pencil cases to school, or that teen girls would be vying to take their tops off for little more than a moment of "fame"?

Some feminists argue that this increased acceptance of "raunch culture"[2] by young women is detrimental and a kind of faux empowerment—and they certainly make valid points. After all, selling a commercialized sexuality to women—one that's overwhelmingly targeted toward getting just the guys off—as a way to be "liberated" is pretty lame.

But I think that while the fast-growing focus on sexuality certainly has the potential to be dangerous for young women, it's not necessarily all bad. What is bad is that young women seem to be confronted with too few choices and too

Target was once blasted for selling padded bras meant for six-year-old girls.

many wagging fingers. Do I think that plucking and waxing, stripping and sucking is inherently feminist? Of course not. But that doesn't mean I think it's inherently wrong or unfeminist either. We're all trapped by the limiting version of sexuality that's put out there—a sexuality that caters almost exclusively to men. And we do the best we can. What irks me is the assumption that any decision young women make is wrong or uninformed.

If we don't approve of the porn culture that tells us our only value is in our ability to be sexy, we're prudes. If we accept it and embrace it, we're sluts. There's no middle ground to be seen. Sound familiar?

What it comes down to is that people don't trust young women. Sure, we make mistakes. I've made plenty. But chastising younger women and telling us that we're making bad decisions isn't helpful. What's important is that we try to understand *why* we're making the decisions we do and how they're related to what we see around us. Like, do we *really* want to flash our boobs (and if so, cool), or are we doing it out of some fucked-up desire to please someone else? Just saying.

Obviously, a huge part of all this is what is expected of young women sexually—that's what pop culture is built on in a tremendous way. And unfortunately, that expectation is kind of like a big old fake orgasm—it's all performance for the sake of the other person, and it often ends up making the real thing harder to get in the end.

That said, I do have faith that younger women can look at pop culture and analyze it in a way that's positive. We may not be able to escape the porn/pop culture ridiculousness, but we can try to use it to create a more reality-based sexuality for ourselves.

That's (Not) Hot

It's pretty well established that girls want to be considered hot. I mean, when you're brought up to think that your hotness quotient is pretty much your entire worth, that shit becomes pretty damn important. Don't get me wrong, I think wanting to be desired is a really understandable thing. Who doesn't want to be wanted? The problem is *who* defines "hot"—and therefore desirability. Hint: It's not women.

Unattainable beauty standards for women aren't a new thing. Magazines, TV shows, and movies have been shoving a certain kind of woman down our throats for decades. White, skinny waist, big boobs, long legs, full lips, great hair—a conglomeration of body parts put together to create the "perfect" woman we're all supposed to be. And if we're not, we're scorned. Nothing worse than being the ugly girl, right?

But it's not just looks that make you "hot"—beauty standards are a whole other conversation. It's being accessible—to men, in particular. To be truly hot in this never-never land of tits and ass, we have to be constantly available—to be looked at, touched, and fucked. Sounds harsh, I know, but it's true. We're only as hot as our willingness to put on a show for guys.

And the "show" is everywhere. In magazines like *Maxim* and *Playboy*. And in the insanity of *Girls Gone Wild*, with teens putting on fake lesbian make-out sessions so guys will think they're hot. We're on display—everywhere. We couldn't escape it if we wanted to. (And maybe some of us don't. More on this later.)

Hot and available is everywhere. *Maxim* magazine—kind of like *Playboy* with more clothes—is the number-one best-selling men's magazine in the nation. *Maxim* not only puts out an annual "hot list" (just in case you forgot how you don't measure up), but also has a VH1 special and is in talks to start *Maxim* hotels and lounges.

Playboy is even worse. All you have to do is go to the local mall to see how normalized *Playboy* has become in American culture. Teens buy *Playboy* shirts before they even have boobs. The E! channel has a reality show, *The Girls Next Door*, based on the lives of several *Playboy* Bunnies who are also magazine founder Hugh Hefner's live-in "girl-friends." MTV has even featured teenagers getting plastic surgery in order to look like (and be) *Playboy* Bunnies. And again—*Playboy* pencil cases. 'Nuff said.

But there's probably no better example of Porn Gone Wild in pop culture than the ubiquitous *Girls Gone Wild (GGW)*. What started as voyeuristic porn lite—girls flashing their boobs to cameras during Mardi Gras and spring break—is now an empire. The company that owns *GGW* claims $40 million in yearly sales, and the founder, Joe Francis, has said he's working on a film, *GGW* ocean cruises, a clothing line, and a restaurant chain (I'm imagining Hooters Gone Wild).

When people think of the way porn culture has oozed into the mainstream in recent years, *Girls Gone Wild* is usually the first thing to come up. After all, *GGW* is where porn meets real life—you don't have to be a porn star to be in one of its videos. You just have to be willing.

I remember the first time I saw one of *GGW*'s late-night commercials, featuring girls lifting their shirts to reveal Mardi Gras beads and little else—maybe a *GGW* logo across their nipples. (Classy, right?) This was back when the girls featured were still largely unaware that their images would be used to make up a tit montage. I mean, really, these were girls who were "caught" on camera in a drunken moment—not girls who sought out the camera breasts first. I felt bad for them; I even recognized a couple of girls. I had gone to Tulane University in New Orleans my freshman year of college; my classmates' getting drunk and flashing on Bourbon Street wasn't exactly out of the ordinary. And while tourists were around and there were the occasional camera flashes, I don't think anyone figured their momentary drunk exhibitionism would be forever captured on film to be sold on a mass scale.

But now girls are lining up to be part of *Girls Gone Wild*—flashing their breasts (and more), masturbating, and having girl-on-girl action, all for fifteen minutes of fame and maybe a *Girls Gone Wild* hat or thong. I'm not going to lie—this bothers the shit out of me. I mean, why in the world would you potentially ruin the rest of your life just so—for a minute—some guy thinks you're hot?

Ariel Levy, who wrote the popular *Female Chauvinist Pigs: Women and the Rise of Raunch Culture*, argues that a new generation of feminists (ahem) is objectifying ourselves and each other by participating in things like *GGW*.

You see, Levy is part of a group of feminist thinkers who aren't too pleased with some of the theory coming from younger feminists—some of whom say that things like sex work or stripping can be empowering, because it's subversive or because hey, it's fun. We're making the choice to participate; therefore, it's powerful. But Levy says that the joke is on us, and that we're really just fooling ourselves.

Maybe.

I understand why *GGW* is so controversial (or *Maxim* and *Playboy*, for that matter). And like I said, it really fucking

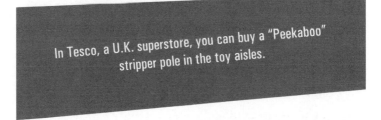

In Tesco, a U.K. superstore, you can buy a "Peekaboo" stripper pole in the toy aisles.

bothers me. But the assumption that *all* girls who enjoy the "show" are stupid or being fooled bothers me just as much. Not to mention that for a lot of women, developing a sexual identity is a process.

In response to Levy's book, Jennifer Baumgardner, third-wave feminist icon and coauthor of *Manifesta*, brought up a supergood point that I think resonates with a lot of women.

❋ If pressed, I'd venture that at least half of my sexual experiences make me cringe when I think about them today. Taking top honors is the many times I made out with female friends in bars when I was in my early twenties, a rite of passage Levy much disdains throughout the book. I'm embarrassed about the kiss-around-the-circles, but if I didn't have those moments, I'm not sure I ever would have found my way to the real long-term relationship I have today. If all my sexual behavior had to be evolved and reciprocal and totally revolutionary before I had it, I'd never have had sex.[3]

Ain't that the truth. I've had more than a couple of embarrassing moments in my life and sexual history—but isn't that what makes us who we are? Do we really have to be on point and thinking politics *all* the time? Sometimes doing silly, disempowering, sexually vapid things when you're young is just part of getting to the good stuff.

I guess what I've come to—and this is what works for me—is that you have to find your own middle ground. There has to be space for young women to figure shit out on their own. And I think most times young women do figure it out.

In a recent Salon.com article about the trend of straight girls making out with each other for male attention, one young woman came to an epiphany while talking to reporter Whitney Joiner:

❋ "A lot of girls who do want long-term boyfriends will still settle for the hookup because it gives them that temporary feeling of being taken care of and being close to someone," Julie says. "It's sad to see that this is what it's come to—that guys will raise the bar and girls will scramble to meet it. Women just want to know what they have to do to get these guys to fall in love with them. And if guys will take them home after kissing a girl, then that's what they're going to do, because it's better than going home alone." She pauses. "Now that I'm saying it out loud, I'm like, Huh—that's a sad way of going about it."[4]

See? I really think it doesn't take all that much for us to work through the pop culture nonsense—we just have to talk it out, hopefully with each other and with women who have been there and done that. Okay, so maybe it won't be quite *that* easy. But it's a start. And it's a much better alternative than calling each other sluts, that's for damn sure.

Like a Virgin, and Other Pop Contradictions

Never mind trying to find an authentic sexuality in our fake-orgasm pop culture—it's near impossible to find *anything* that makes sense. There are all of these contradictions in porn/pop culture that blow my mind and make it all the more difficult for young women to find an authentic sexual identity. It hurts the head to talk about them too much, but unfortunately it's necessary if we really want to get a grasp on what is being expected of women: the impossible.

BE A VIRGIN . . . BUT BE SEXY

We already know that we're supposed to be virginal (lest we mar our purity), but when it comes to pop culture, the virginity thing gets more complicated. Since I'd probably date myself by talking about Madonna's "Like a Virgin," I won't go there. Think Britney Spears (pre-K-Fed) and Jessica Simpson (pre-*Newlyweds*). They both claimed to be "saving themselves" for marriage and spoke out against premarital sex (while simultaneously presenting themselves in the most sexual way possible, of course). Naturally, it later came out that Spears (before her two weddings) had sex; it was rumored that Simpson managed to wait till the night before her wedding. I can't think of a better example of how we expect girls to be sexy but not have sex. It's the *idea* of virginity

In 2006, the British government banned violent pornography.

that's popular, not the reality of being chaste. Look sexy, act as if you're having sex, but if you do it . . . whore! You can even look at the newfound popularity of "revirginization" surgeries—you know, getting your hymen "repaired." It's the lie and the performance of being a virgin, not the reality. Truly baffling. And impossible to recreate. Unless you feel like getting a new hymen.

BE AVAILABLE . . . BUT UNATTAINABLE

Like I mentioned earlier about hotness: It's about accessibility. We're expected to be available to men, but we're also expected to be "mysterious." Much in the same way we're supposed to be sexy but not give it up. Think about a *Maxim* cover girl—she's totally unattainable but simultaneously available for consumption. No guy who reads the magazine will ever meet her or talk to her—but he gets to look at her half-naked and jerk off to her if he wants, which is something he can't always get from the women he meets in his everyday life. So in that way, she's the "perfect" girl. Again, impossible for real women to live up to.

LIKE SEX . . . BUT DON'T COME

The prevalence of porn has led to this really weird point in American society where the sexual ideal for younger women is a porn star. Internet porn and the normalization of pornography have spawned a whole new generation of guys who were raised thinking that porn sex equals normal sex. Not to mention a generation of girls who think porn sex is the only way to please guys. So we're expected to—once again—put on the "show." This means a whole load of screaming, dirty-talking, and sex-loving madness. But the problem is that we're expected to imitate something that's *acted*. Most porn stars aren't really getting off. So the best sex is fake sex? Think about what this does to younger people trying to develop their sexuality! Terrifying.

BE A LESBIAN . . . WHO LIKES MEN

Being a lesbian is totally acceptable—so long as there's a man around to watch it—and you're young and "hot," of course. The absence of any real images of lesbians in pop culture is kind of crazy. I mean, even Showtime's *The L Word* features a bevy of sexy gals and storylines that fit pretty neatly into the girl-on-girl male fantasy. This isn't to say that there aren't outed women in the mainstream—there are. But the pop culture, sexed-up version of lesbians is what reigns supreme. Just think of the appropriation of lesbianism by straight male porn. As I mentioned before, there are a ton of young feminists who have thought and written about this in a political frame of mind. By filtering porn/pop through that thought process, I think we can end up in a space where we recognize that while some things are fucked up, there's still room to do things that are fun and powerful. While a lesbian make-out session may be a fake expression of lust to some, it's an awesome, authentic experience to others, so if you want to make out with a girl, go for it. It's about the consciousness behind your decisions. Many younger women *know* what we want and go for it. And that's nothing to apologize for. But if you're doing something you wouldn't normally want to do, or if the only thought behind something sexual is *Please god, let him like me,* you may be in trouble. If you're doing something that mimics someone else's sexual choices—for someone else's benefit or because you feel pressured—then you might want to consider how empowered that choice actually is.

BE A WOMAN OF COLOR . . . BUT ONLY IN STEREOTYPES, PLEASE

Women who aren't white (or at least aren't on the fair side) are nearly invisible in pop culture—unless they're adhering to the most vile racial stereotypes. Sure, *Maxim* or *Playboy* will occasionally feature women of color on their pages, but they're generally as Caucasian-looking as possible. And you don't have to look far for the tired old stereotypes. Black women are bitchy! And if there's an overweight black woman, she's going to be all sassy! Asian women are docile and bow a lot! Latinas are spicy hot hot hot! It's not just in the sexual stereotyping of women of color in magazines—but in television shows, movies, and even porn listings. Actually, if you want the perfect example of this pattern, go to the back pages of a

The world's first Feminist Porn Awards were given in June 2006 in Toronto, Canada.

local paper that has escort-service ads. You will undoubtedly see ads of black women that are all ass shots ("Big Booty!"), ads of Asian women who are all shy ("Lotus Flowers!"), and ads of white girls touted as college gals ("All American!"). So many stereotypes, so little time. But truly, just the fact that women of color are pretty much invisible in pop culture speaks volumes.

What all of these contradictions add up to are insanely impossible expectations of women. (And yes, I'm aware that pop culture puts expectations on men as well. But really, not like it does on women.) These baffling expectations mean that any authentic expression of yourself is near impossible. How do you act like yourself when you're constantly putting on a show?

Performance vs. Reality

Contradictions aside, what all this porn/pop culture has in common is performance. Sometimes performance can be a cool thing when it comes to sexuality.

Rachel Kramer Bussel, a feminist sex columnist at *The Village Voice*, says that younger women are claiming a public space for their sexuality.

> ❋ I think we have to move beyond the overly simplis-
> tic "empowered" or "exploited" debate. We can
> acknowledge that our motivations for putting our
> bodies "out there" may not be the same as what's ta
> ken away by certain consumers, but we wrestle with

and confront those contradictions. Instead of attacking women for the choices they make, we should be working toward creating a more accepting, welcoming culture that values sexual diversity. I see many positive signs that sexual culture is flourishing and thriving among the younger generation in ways that are more egalitarian, open, and honest, whether it's indie porn magazine *Sweet Action*, the many college sex magazines and columns, or the thriving burlesque scenes happening across the country which celebrate curvy girls, striptease, double entendre, and sexuality. Some even have male dancers and you can really see with the new burlesque how "sexy" does not have to equal "exploited." Sexy can be aggressive, alluring, entertaining, and even thought-provoking all at once.[5]

The difference between what Rachel is talking about—in my opinion—and stuff like *Girls Gone Wild* is that some performances are thought out and some are, well, not. (Especially when you consider the inebriation factor for those less-thought-out times.)

Can a performance really be a subversive way of playing with your sexuality? Sure. But I think it's a really individual thing and depends on how much you're buying in to the bullshit notions of what sexy is. Rachel is clearly not buying in.

And again, if you want to show your tits just for the pure fun of it—go for it. But I do think it's incredibly important that we always be aware of *why* we want to do certain things.

So What's a Girl to Do?

It shouldn't be that hard to develop an authentic sexuality— or even personhood, for that matter. But the prevalence of porn/pop makes it pretty frigging difficult to negotiate how we separate good kinds of performance from bad and how we develop an identity that isn't mired in all of this ridiculous crap.

Some suggestions that have worked for me:

STOP GETTING SO DRUNK

I'm well aware that going out and partying is fun. Shit, I have a hangover as I'm writing this. But my college years taught me well about drinking and participating in sexual activities (whether it's actual sex, flashing, make-out sessions, whatever). If you wouldn't do it sober, don't do it drunk. 'Cause I guarantee if it's something that really turns you on, it will be more fun sober. Plus, if you're sober, you can't use the liquor as an excuse for your actions—because, again, if it's fun and something you want to do, you shouldn't have to make excuses. Ever. (And let's be honest—binge drinking is très gross.)

ARE YOU HAVING FUN?

Serious fun. Not "this seems like a good idea" fun. And definitely not "well, they're egging me on" non-fun. So much of our personalities get caught up in trying to adhere to what we're "supposed" to be like, it's hard to just, you know, relax. When you're trying to be sexy, virginal, available but not, appropriately lesbian but still straight, skinny, hot, and so on, all of a sudden life ain't so fun anymore. It takes a lot of work to remain in pop culture character. So make it easy on yourself—if it's not fun, fuck it.

DOES IT FEEL GOOD?

Yeah, I'm dirty. But you get what I'm saying. Because I really can't imagine that whole porn-performance thing is too orgasm friendly—after all, performing *does* mean faking it.

WHY DO YOU WANT IT?

Obviously, everything we do is affected to a certain degree by social norms and what pop culture demands of us. I think it's fine to go along with these things to a certain extent, so long as you're always cognizant of why you're doing it. For example, I wear makeup. I love it. But I recognize that the reason I love it sooo much is that the larger world tells me I need it to be pretty. Would it be revolutionary of me to throw all of my makeup away? Yup. But I don't want to. I wear it, but I'm aware of why I do.

But Sometimes You Just Can't Win

Unfortunately, despite our best efforts to work through all of these expectations for ourselves, we're always going to be judged. If we adhere to the porn/pop standard, we're sluts (or dumb), even if we've come to a place where we're comfortable with our actions. I don't say this to be a downer, I just think it's important to recognize how the same society that enforces these standards will use them against us whenever it can. And in really dangerous ways.

There was a case in California—and you'll hear more about this in Chapter 4, "The Blame (and Shame) Game"— where a teen girl's gang rape was videotaped. The defense team said oh no, she just wanted to make a "porn" video. And that logic flew—because the idea of a girl putting on a "show" is pretty normal. You know, 'cause girls just love to go wild and get raped on video.[6]

This kind of blaming also comes up a lot with the idea of "girls behaving badly"—as in spring break, going out and hooking up, and other things that we've been taught are fun rites of passage. For example, the American Medical Association (AMA) released a poll in 2006 about all of the debaucherous spring-break activities going on—like promiscuity and binge drinking.[7] The funny thing? It was specific to women. Because apparently we're the only ones who drink and hook up.

The poll of young women (seventeen to thirty-five years old) showed that 83 percent of those surveyed drank most of the nights while on spring break; 74 percent said spring break results in increased sexual activity. (Is this really news?) I'm all for curbing binge drinking and the dumb *GGW* expectations of spring break, but I can't help but be irked that this finger-wagging is only pointed at young women. 'Cause you really can't tell me that men on spring break don't drink too much and have sex. But the AMA's main concern was that girls are having too much sex. But . . . but . . . I thought that's what "hot" girls did! So annoying. Conservative groups *loved* this study and used it to argue that girls who go out and party are just asking to be raped. Seriously. Janice Crouse, a spokesperson from Concerned Women for America, said in an interview:

☀ What we find is the whole culture is really encouraging girls to be more wild. For instance, *Playboy* is saying, you know, girls need to be more rebellious, a bit more out there in your face, a bit more like the guys. To be a prude or someone who is straight-laced is the worst thing you can do. . . . So I think it's high time the AMA and the government got into the business of warning young women, and saying to them this is not just something that's dangerous to your health, it's dangerous to your life.[8]

Basically, she's saying that if girls are out socializing and having fun, they're putting themselves in danger. By doing exactly what society tells us girls are supposed to do, we're leaving ourselves open to being raped and murdered

The problem is, there are people who *will* use this as an excuse for violent behavior against women. I don't think it's coincidental that Joe Francis, the founder of *GGW,* has been accused of rape on numerous occasions (of the very girls who are going wild). But trying to pretend that if we somehow didn't follow pop culture standards, all would be fine and dandy . . . bullshit.

The same society that puts forth these narrow views of women in pop culture also thinks we're expendable, that we're good only for one thing—men's enjoyment.

So remember, this is definitely a screwed-if-you-do, screwed-if-you-don't situation. You just remember to say, "Screw them."

Survivor

4

THE BLAME (AND SHAME) GAME

I wish I could write an update to this chapter and be able to say that sexual assault and victim-blaming has gone the way of the dodo. But I can't. Because despite righteous activism by feminists and antiviolence advocates, we're just not there yet. We still live in a country where more than 600,000 adult women (that number increases when you count those under eighteen) were raped in 2010, and where blaming women for someone assaulting them is still the norm.

In fact, if anything, the last few years have shown us just how rape illiterate (a term I coined in *The Nation*) our country actually is. In the months leading up to the 2012 presidential election, an inordinate number of male politicians made bizarre—but telling—comments about sexual assault. In an Indiana Senate debate, Republican Richard Mourdock said he opposes abortion with no exceptions because pregnancy from rape is "something that God intended." Before that, Missouri politician Todd Akin told a local television reporter that women can't get pregnant if it's a "legitimate rape" (are there rapes that aren't legitimate?!) because "the female body has ways to try to shut that whole thing down." In 2011, Wisconsin state representative Roger Rivard told a reporter that "some girls rape easy." These weren't just gaffes—this is what our culture thinks about rape and this is why, combined with a nice dose of misogyny, so many people still think that rape is somehow women's fault.

Thankfully, feminists are holding these men—and this culture—accountable for the various ways in which they support rape culture. But until Americans fully understand what rape actually is—until we have a widespread, culturally accepted definition of rape that takes into account structural inequities—we will continue to see more of the same.

Violence against women is at epidemic levels in the United States. Sexual assault, intimate partner violence, harassment, and stalking are part of many women's daily lives. Young women are particularly affected by violence—we are more likely to be assaulted and less likely to get help. Why are we not freaking out about this?

Violence against women is *so* common that it's become a normal part of our lives. And it's being committed by "normal" people. If you are raped, the guy's not likely to be some random dude jumping out of the bushes. He will be your friend, a guy you know from school, a friend's brother, someone at a party. That's what scares me most about rapists—they're otherwise regular guys, some of whom don't understand that what they've done is wrong, others of whom don't care. Young men in the United States have been brought up to think that they have open access to women's bodies and sexuality. Everything in American culture tells men that women are there for *them,* there for sex, constantly available. It breeds a society where rape is expected and practically okayed. So long as men are being brought up to think that violence and sexual assault are okay, this isn't just women's problem.

Yeah, I know, all of a sudden I'm not so jokey. This one hits home for me. I spent about a year (because that's all I could take) volunteering as an emergency room advocate for survivors of sexual assault and domestic violence. If someone went to the emergency room after being assaulted—and this included women, men, and kids—I would go in and stay with them while they were in the hospital and try to make their time there as smooth as possible. It's one thing to hear about rape statistics or to talk about domestic violence as some faraway, abstract thing. When it's in your face—or in your life—the reality of violence is overwhelming. This is something that we can't let devolve into another after-school-special issue that people talk about but don't address head on.

Violence against women is one of those things that we kinda deal with all the time, but not in a substantive way. I mean, how many TV movies will you see (Lifetime addicts, I'm talking to you!) in which women are victims of rape or domestic violence? Shit, there are television shows dedicated to addressing the horror of sexual crimes—think *Law & Order SVU*. We have V-Day, a reinterpretation of Valentine's Day, when organizations bring attention to violence against women on Valentine's Day. We're taught about rape in school. Domestic violence *is* a well-known problem. It's not like these are issues that people *don't* know about. So you would think that we would be making leaps and bounds in dealing with violence against women. But it's just the opposite. We're so accustomed to seeing violence against women that it's become normalized. We accept it as an inevitable fact of life, rather than an epidemic that we need to fight on a large scale. And that's not okay.

Rape/Sexual Assault

When I was in college, a teacher once said that all women live by a "rape schedule." I was baffled by the term, but as she went on to explain, I got really freaked out. Because I realized that I knew exactly what she was talking about. And you do too. Because of their constant fear of rape (conscious or not), women do things throughout the day to protect themselves. Whether it's carrying our keys in our hands as we walk home, locking our car doors as soon as we get in, or not walking down certain streets, we take precautions. While taking precautions is certainly not a bad idea, the fact that certain things women do are so ingrained into our daily routines is truly disturbing. It's essentially like living in a prison—all the time. We can't assume that we're safe anywhere: not on the streets, not in our homes. And we're so used to feeling unsafe that we don't even see that there's something seriously fucked up about it.

Perhaps the most screwed-up thing about women living by a "rape schedule" is that it's not all that effective. We assume that if we're going to be attacked, it will be by some random crazy jumping from behind a tree. But, as I mentioned, that's just not the case. According to a 2004 National Crime Victimization Survey, almost two-thirds of all rapes are committed by someone the victim knows: a relative, an

In 2006, Bush appointed Mary Beth Buchanan to head the Office on Violence Against Women, whose claim to fame was spending $12 million on prosecuting people who sold bongs So yeah, real qualified.

acquaintance, a friend—even a lover.[1] Perhaps you've heard this before, but I think it's too important not to repeat. Because this is the statistic that shows just how "normal" rape is in the United States. It makes us feel better to think that we're safe, that we're okay if we protect ourselves from the boogeyman perv on the subway or in the bushes. Maybe it's just too difficult to acknowledge that as it stands, we're not safe anywhere. Yeah, I'm a downer. And I'm not done.

That same government study shows that every two and a half minutes, someone is sexually assaulted in the United

States, and that one in six women has been the victim of an attempted or completed rape. (Keep in mind, rape is one of the most underreported crimes, so that statistic is likely too low.) For young women, the numbers are even worse. Eighty percent of rape victims are under thirty years old; 44 percent are under eighteen. Even worse, young women are much less likely to get help if they've been assaulted.

This is partly because some women don't even realize that they've been raped. I know that sounds bizarre, but it's true. We've bought in to the whole guys-deserving-access-to-women thing, too. Some women think that if force wasn't used, it wasn't rape. Some women think that they "deserved" it. Or that they "owed" a guy sex. 'Cause he bought her dinner or something. I shit you not.

So what *is* rape, anyway? Not to get all technical and educator-ish—because I'm well aware that plenty of women know all this—but it's worth going over.

The legal definition differs from state to state, but the generally accepted definition is forced intercourse (vaginal, anal, or oral)—force being physical or psychological coercion. Men can be raped. Rape is not always heterosexual; women can rape women, men can rape men.

Sexual assault is different. It's unwanted sexual contact, like grabbing, fondling, or other nasties. (I'm thinking of the douchebag on the subway when I was in high school who rubbed up against me. Shudder.)

I think the hardest thing to understand about rape and sexual assault is how—after we've supposedly come so far—

it still happens and we're so quick to excuse it. After years of legislation, awareness-raising, and activism, women are still being blamed for being the victims of violent crimes.

Blaming the Victim

You would think that in this day and age, blaming the victim would be long gone. If only we were so lucky. Here are just a few of the common rape-blaming techniques. (They come in handy during rape trials.)

WEARING A SKIRT EQUALS OPEN FOR BUSINESS

The outfit argument is one that never seems to get old. It's been around forever, but it may be the most bizarre victim-blaming tactic of them all. Here's the idea: If you're wearing something that could be considered "slutty," like (gasp!) a skirt, you were asking to be raped. Or you were teasing those poor guys who just can't help themselves (they learned that in abstinence ed, remember?). This never made sense to me on so many levels, but I imagine that guys must find it pretty insulting. It basically means that they're just big, dumb animals unable to control themselves within one hundred yards of a miniskirt. I don't know about you, but I think we should give men some credit. Not to mention we should be able to wear whatever the fuck we want without fear of rape. Even more strange? Your outfit doesn't even have to be revealing for you to be blamed for it. A supreme court in Italy actually overturned a rape conviction because the victim was wearing jeans. The argument was that she must have agreed to sex because her jeans couldn't have been removed without her help.[2] Yeah.

GIRLS JUST WANT TO HAVE FUN

Another fave blaming tactic is the "impaired" argument. So if you're drunk or otherwise fucked up, you're not to be trusted. Or you should have seen it coming. I remember seeing one of those anti-drug commercials a while back that was *supposed* to be about marijuana. It showed a house party where a young-ish teen girl was smoking pot. It then showed her passing out on a couch and a creepy-looking guy coming to sit down next to her. He looks around and then starts to put his hand down her shirt. The screen fades out and you hear the girl say "no" in kind of a whisper. Here's the kicker: After the screen fades out, the message says, "Marijuana lowers your inhibitions." Huh? But *she* was the one smoking, so I guess *her* inhibitions were lowered enough to be passed out and assaulted? Yeah, victim-blaming at its government-funded best.

Another example: A writer for *The Wall Street Journal*, Naomi Schaefer Riley, wrote a piece on the rape and murder of New York college student Imette St. Guillen. Riley wrote that the student "was last seen in a bar, alone and drinking at 3 AM," and that "a twenty-four-year-old woman should know better."[3] I guess St. Guillen wasn't aware of the woman-only curfew and alcohol prohibition. Do you really want to live in a world where someone is going to blame you for being raped (and murdered!) just for going to a bar and getting a drink? This isn't to say that women shouldn't be aware of how alcohol and drugs can affect them. Of course we should try to be as safe as possible. But the focus needs to be on the perpetrator—not women.

NO HYMEN, NO RAPE

God help you if you've been raped and you're not a virgin. Because apparently if you've slept with one guy, you want to sleep with them all. Remember our friend Bill Napoli on the only girl who should be able to get an abortion? The sodomized virgin? It's kind of like that. An Italian court ruled in February 2006 that sexual abuse is less serious if the girl isn't a virgin.[4] Seriously. Now, obviously your sexual history has *nothing* to do with sexual assault, but somehow it's always brought up. A study in the United Kingdom showed that a third of people believe that a woman is partially or totally

Just so you know: April is Sexual Assault Awareness month, and October is Domestic Violence Awareness month.

responsible for being raped if she has been "flirtatious," and one in five think she's responsible if she's had "many" sexual partners![5] In a case in California where a teen girl's gang rape was videotaped, the defense team called her "trash" and a slut who wanted to make a "porn" video.[6] Never mind that she was unconscious. Never mind that she was raped with a pool cue, a lit cigarette, a can, and a Snapple bottle. Never mind that during the attack, passed out, she urinated on herself. At the end of the first trial, the case was put on hold because of a hung jury.[7] Now tell me that the slut-baiting doesn't work. If you don't fit into the "good girl" standard—or if people can convince others that you don't—you're in real trouble. If you're a stripper, prepare to be disbelieved. If you're a prostitute, forget it.

WOMEN SHOULD KNOW BETTER (MY PERSONAL FAVORITE)

This is the ultimate in victim-blaming: the all-encompassing "She should have known better." Known better than to wear a skirt. Known better than to walk home alone. Known better than to be drinking. Known better than to be alone with a guy. The real danger of this whopper is that it plays on the guilt that rape victims feel—and that's seriously fucked up. Not to mention, it pretty much ignores the rapist. It assumes that rape is inevitable, and that the onus should be on women to protect ourselves. What about the folks doing the raping? I guess they're off the hook. Women (and men) have to know that there is nothing you can do that warrants being raped. Nothing. I don't care if you're a naked, drunk, passed-out prostitute. It doesn't matter.

Thankfully, the rates of sexual assault are dropping (thanks in part to legislation enacted by feminists), but the culture of rape we live in keeps on trucking. This is one of the reasons feminism is so important. This isn't about random acts of violence. This is about young men being brought up to look at women as less than human. Seriously, dehumanization is what makes people able to commit violence against each other.

That California rape case? Thankfully, guilty verdicts were handed down eventually. But the damage done to the young woman was irrevocable; she was completely dehumanized by the rape and by the legal system. Check out her statement to the judge.

> ☀ I cannot and don't think I will ever be able to describe what I felt while watching that video. I remember asking myself, *When did I become a piece of meat and not a human being to these men?* They did things not even savage animals would do. They violated me in every way possible. . . . I was like a lifeless and feelingless doll that these men thought they could use and abuse in any way they wished.[8]

It's easy to get angry; this is some horrible stuff. But we need to look past the anger and ask some tough questions. The young men who raped this woman were people she thought were her friends. They were teenagers. What kind of culture are we living in that breeds guys who think this is reasonable, even cool, behavior?

What to Do, What to Do?

A term that's used by a lot of feminists and other folks to describe this fucked-upness is "rape culture." We live in a culture that essentially condones rape. Yeah, it's illegal, but social and political conditions implicitly "allow for" rape. Like, how many men actually go to jail for rape? How many women are still blamed? Besides, you can't tell me this isn't a cultural problem when at least one in six women will be the victim of an attempted or completed rape! Those aren't small numbers—this is a huge problem, and it's time we started treating it as such.

The problem is, too many "solutions" put the impetus for change on women—like safety measures. A woman in South Africa, for example, invented an anti-rape device for women in response to the high rates of sexual assault in her country. The device, which is kind of like a female condom (you have to wear it inside your vagina), will fold around the perpetrator's penis and attach itself with microscopic hooks.[9] It's impossible to remove without medical help. Now, sounds like justice

> The South Carolina House Judiciary Committee voted in 2005 to make cockfighting a felony, but tabled a bill that would have done the same for domestic violence.

for a rapist asshole, I know. But the problem is this: It's up to the woman to protect herself against a rapist. It's *our* job to make sure that we don't get raped, not men's responsibility to make sure that they don't attack women. (And, of course, the device is problematic because women can be raped orally and anally, and I'm guessing putting hooks in a guy's dick will probably make him pretty violent.) Women across the United States will take self-defense classes or carry safety whistles. They'll put pepper spray in their purses and walk fast through parking lots. All good things, I guess. But we can't keep running away. We should be able to walk the streets—or stay at home, for that matter—without fearing violence.

Intimate Partner Violence

Most people are familiar with the term domestic violence, but intimate partner violence (IPV) is a newer term. When people think of domestic violence, they generally think of a boyfriend and girlfriend or a husband and wife. But violence can happen in any kind of relationship. IPV broadens the definition. It's physical or emotional abuse by a partner, wife, husband, boyfriend, girlfriend, an ex, or a date.

IPV affects both men and women, but women are disproportionately the victims of violence in relationships. Women make up 85 percent of the victims of IPV, and one-third of American women report being physically or sexually assaulted by a partner (husband, boyfriend, whoever) at some point in their lives. Again, the numbers are even scarier for young women. One report says that 40 percent of teenage girls say they know someone their age who has been hit by a boyfriend. That's just out of control.

And the truly scary thing about IPV is that it's rarely an isolated incident. Violence in relationships tends to follow a pattern—a cycle of abuse. Sounds technical, I know. Most people think of domestic violence in kind of a stereotypical way—a guy slapping around his girlfriend when he's had too much to drink, for example. But the truth is a lot more complicated than that.

The cycle starts with a "tension-building phase," where—duh—tension builds between the couple. There could be emotional and verbal and physical abuse during this time. When the tension reaches a climax, there is an incident of physical abuse on a larger scale—the tension is so high at this point that anything can trigger it. After the incident, the batterer moves on to the "honeymoon" phase, where there are apologies, excuses—"I'll change" and such (cough, bullshit, cough). Then the cycle begins again. And again. Often, the violent incidents will get worse over time.

There's also a pattern when it comes to those who abuse their partners. There are definite warning signs. The weird thing? A lot of potentially abusive men initially come off as the "perfect" guy. They are immediately superromantic and want to spend all their time with you. But this is often the abusers' setting the stage so they can take total control of the relationship by creating an atmosphere in which they're the biggest thing in your life. Because then it's harder to leave, of course.

Some signs of a potentially abusive partner:

- **Isolation:** They tell you that they don't want you to spend time with your friends or your family because they want to see you all the time. Later, this can turn into the abuser's trying to block access to transportation (messing up your car), work (deliberately making you late), or other modes of communication with people outside the relationship.

- ☀ **Jealousy:** Sometimes a little jealousy makes a gal feel wanted, but abusers go above and beyond. They may become jealous at the drop of a hat or even resent time spent with anyone besides them—even family members.

- ☀ **Control:** This is the key; it's all about control. Abusers control their partner's ability to come and go, to spend money, to make decisions. They want to control everything.

Other signs/abusive actions include enforcing seriously traditional gender roles (in which men expect their female partners to do all the nurturing and taking care of their every need), verbally abusing their partner, using force during sex or being sexually manipulative, using cruelty to animals or kids as a means to control their partner's behavior . . . the list goes on.

I guess my point is, there's a lot more to violent relationships than individual incidents. Some abusers may never even leave a mark on their victims. A nurse once told me of a man who would force his wife to drink Tabasco sauce as a punishment. It's about control and fear—and violence is just a means to the end.

VICTIM-BLAMING

Victim-blaming happens constantly when it comes to relationship violence, mostly because of one question: Why don't they leave? The answer is that it's really never that simple. Here are some of the most common reasons victims stay in abusive relationships:

* **Poverty:** Many women lack the financial resources to leave; in fact, 60 percent of female welfare recipients have been victims of relationship violence. They have no place to go, and they may have children. Their partner may have taken control of their bank accounts, ensured that property is only listed under the abuser's name, and so on. It's not so easy to leave when you don't have a dollar to your name.

* **Isolation:** Once women have been isolated from their friends and family, they may not have any support system left.

* **Fear of increased violence/death:** Most women who are killed by their partners are in the process of leaving or planning to leave. Many women know that if they try to leave and fail, the violent consequences could be lethal.

* **Cultural/religious beliefs:** Some women's culture or religion tells them that divorce isn't okay, or that violence is acceptable. They may fear being ostracized by their family and community.

So again, not so simple. And I can't emphasize this enough: We have to get beyond the idea that it's *our* responsibility to not have violence done to us. We deserve to be safe in our relationships.

HARASSMENT

You *know* you have a favorite street-harassment story. (And yeah, I know there's harassment at work and such; we'll get into that in another chapter.)

The first time I saw a penis was when some random dude on a subway platform took his out and started running toward me with it. Charming, huh? Talk about a scarring experience. I just froze. Luckily, a train came into the station and he just got on like nothing had happened. Then there was the guy who told me my ass looked so good he wanted to eat his dinner off it. (You think that line ever worked?) Then, just recently, I walked past a young man in front of the New York City library and he leaned over and whispered, "I want to eat you" in my ear. I actually felt his breath on me—nasty.

I'm sure you have your stories, too. We all do. For some reason (ahem, rape culture), guys think that they have the right to say anything to you. Or grab your ass. It's the assumption that you're there solely for them. One essay, "The Little Rapes, Sexual Harassment" by authors Andrea Medea and Kathleen Thompson, makes the connection between street harassment and rape.[10] They're both intrusions into your personal space, your right to just *be*. Both harassment and rape are the results of a culture that teaches men that women exist solely for them, their desires.

WHAT THEY DON'T TELL YOU

Too often, issues of violence against women are presented in a pretty universal way. The white woman being beat by her no-good, drunk husband. It's got "movie of the week" written all over it. What's shown less often in the media (or anywhere else, for that matter) is violence in the lives of women who aren't white, middle-class, straight gals. Obviously these issues affect all women, regardless of their race, class, and sexual orientation—but some women are affected disproportionately.

For example, African American women are much less likely to report a rape. Native American women are most likely to be raped by a white offender. Sixty-one percent of female soldiers have said they have been sexually harassed in the army. Queer women are more likely to be attacked than straight women. Women on welfare are more likely to be victims of domestic violence.

Race, class, sexual orientation—or even the kind of job or career a woman has—influence how violence affects her.

THE LAWS THAT MAKE IT BETTER, THE LAWS THAT MAKE YOU WANT TO SCREAM

It's amazing to me how the United States can simultaneously have great and shitty laws concerning violence against women.

Probably the most important piece of legislation is the Violence Against Women Act (VAWA). It gives billions of dollars to help survivors of rape, intimate partner violence, and stalking. What's weird is that more people don't know about it. It passed in 1994 and was reauthorized in 2000, 2005, and 2006. This latest reauthorization extended VAWA for five more years and increased funding—VAWA now allocates $3.9 billion to related state and federal programs. Impressive, right? Unfortunately, there are folks who actually want it done away with. Bush has tried to cut VAWA funding substantially (shocker, I know), and other organizations that call themselves "men's rights activists" speak out against the law, saying that it discriminates against men (not true—the law allows for funding for men as well). So while VAWA is doing great things, it's still under attack.

There are other laws—mostly state laws—that seriously screw women over when it comes to violence. The gay marriage ban in Ohio, for example, is the perfect example of how all of our rights are interconnected. If one group is fucked, we're all fucked. It's actually getting abusers off

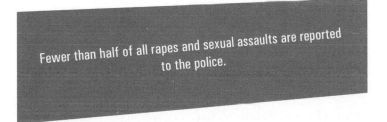

Fewer than half of all rapes and sexual assaults are reported to the police.

the hook. Since the same-sex-marriage ban prohibits legal recognition of any relationship of "unmarried individuals that intends to approximate the design, qualities, significance, or effect of marriage," judges have been ruling that the state domestic violence law doesn't apply to unmarried couples. Yeah. So women who are being beaten by their live-in boyfriends are basically being told that if they want to press domestic violence charges, they'll have to marry their abuser. Sweet, huh?

Other politicians are trying to make it okay for Catholic hospitals to deny rape victims emergency contraception because it goes against their principles. Apparently, the principles of a woman who doesn't want to get pregnant by her rapist don't count.

In Tennessee, it's not illegal for a man to rape his wife unless he "uses a weapon, causes her serious bodily injury, or they are separated or divorcing." When spousal rape does qualify as a crime, it's treated as a less serious crime than a rape of any other woman.

You see what I'm getting at. The fight is far from over.

Taking Action

Hearing all this stuff is really disheartening, I know. But just because culture at large isn't doing all it can to combat violence against women, it doesn't mean women aren't. Women (and men) across the country work their asses off in organizations like the Family Violence Prevention Fund; the Rape, Abuse & Incest National Network; INCITE! Women of Color Against Violence; and Legal Momentum. Not to mention the countless rape crisis centers and domestic violence shelters out there.

And it's not just women working in women's organizations who are making a difference. Young women are getting seriously innovative in their free time.

One New York City website called Holla Back catches street harassers in the act and publishes their pictures online. Readers are encouraged to take pictures of would-be flashers and harassers with their camera phones and send them in with their stories. ("If you can't slap 'em, snap 'em" is their motto. Perfect.)[11]

The organization RightRides, which you learned about in Chapter 1, offers free rides home to women who are out late on the weekends.

There are even organizations dedicated to educating men about violence against women—there aren't a lot of them, but they're there. Men Can Stop Rape is an organization that provides training for younger men and boys on violence and gender equality. We could use a lot more organizations like this. Remember: This is not just women's problem!

And these are just a few examples. Across the country, young women are thinking of new ways to take the battle against violence into their own hands. And you can too. You have to.

MINE

5

IF THESE UTERINE WALLS COULD TALK

Reproductive justice issues have been at the forefront of politics the last few years. From repeated attempts to defund Planned Parenthood, efforts to close any and all abortion clinics, and the continued state-level rollbacks of reproductive rights—a lot has been going on. Some of it has been more of the same—we've seen legislation aimed at sending women back to the '50s in nearly every state in the country. In South Dakota, a bill was introduced that would have legalized killing abortion providers—yes, seriously. The bill said that committing murder in defense of a fetus is justifiable homicide, which opened the door for anyone in that state to kill providers. (The bill went nowhere, thankfully.) In Arizona and in Kansas, Republicans tried to pass a bill that would make it legal to lie to women about prenatal test results to make sure they don't get abortions. So your doctor could keep important medical information from you—if your pregnancy was in danger, if your fetus had a chromosomal abnormality—and that would be legal. Also in Arizona, lawmakers tried to pass a bill that would make it legal for employers to fire women for using birth control, and to mandate that they prove a medical reason for being on birth control, if they're on the Pill. On the federal level, HR358, the ironically named "Protect Life Act," would have allowed hospitals and healthcare providers to deny sick women life-saving abortions. So you could go to a hospital needing an abortion to save your life and not only could they refuse the procedure, they could refuse to transport you to a hospital that would give you an abortion.

This has been par for the course for years. What has changed, however, is online activism. When Susan G. Komen for the Cure tried to stop funding Planned Parenthood, for example, an online furor forced the breast cancer foundation to reverse itself. Similar activism on a Virginia bill that would have mandated invasive transvaginal ultrasounds for women seeking abortions—feminists called it "state rape" on Twitter—resulted in the legislation being amended. There is a shift in the way we respond to attacks on reproductive health that is only getting stronger. And the country is coming with us. Right before the election, a Gallup poll showed that 40 percent of women in swing states named abortion as the most important issue for women in the election. Another poll showed that the majority of Americans—54 percent— are pro-choice. So I'm optimistic that despite the continued assaults, feminists are up for a fight. And we're in it to win.

It's not news that women's reproductive rights are under attack. Shit, by the time I'm done writing this sentence, another state will probably outlaw abortion. And if there's any issue that's associated with feminism, it's abortion. Because feminists eat babies. (Sorry, couldn't help myself.)

Feminist baby-eating aside, repro rights are about more than abortion and birth control. They're about being able to have sex when we want to. They're about having affordable, accessible contraception. They're about being able to control our bodies even if we can't drive a car or vote yet. And if we're feeling parental, they're also about being allowed to have children. Unfortunately, these seemingly reasonable things are a lot more complicated than they should be. Especially for young women.

We don't hear that much about how reproductive rights is a young women's issue. I mean, we *are* the fertile ones, right? Not only are young women more likely to get pregnant, we're also more likely to have restrictions on our contraceptive choices and pregnancy options. That's why it's so important that we be on top of this shit. Repro rights is the one issue that mainstream U.S. women's organizations have been focusing on for a long time—but younger women are at the center of the battle, so we have to take our rightful place in it.

There's something else about women's repro rights that isn't talked about that much—the *real* reason behind the anti-abortion, anti-contraception nonsense. At the heart of it all, it's truly about just hating sex, or at least hating that women have sex. There's a lot of talk about life and morals, but it's nonsense. To the people who want to limit your choices, it's about slut-punishing. They are completely terrified of girls having The Sex. So much so that they'd rather see us pregnant or with an STD than give us the tools to have The Sex safely. Shit, they're even making up bizarre stories about birth control–based teen sex cults (I'm not joking).

If we want anything to change, we can't forget this. Plus, we can make fun of them for being all prudey.

Contraception Misconception

Nothing exemplifies the real motives of the anti-sexers as much as their stance on birth control. They talk a big game about how bad abortion is, but most of them don't say much about contraception. That's because they don't want you to know what they really think—that birth control is bad. They don't want you to use it. Ever. Now why in the world would the people who hate abortion so much want you to forgo the one thing that keeps you from getting pregnant?

HAVING ALL THE GOODIES AND NOT PAYING THE PRICE

Because it's for sluts. Seriously. According to Missouri State Representative Cynthia Davis (who tried to remove a state requirement that sex ed classes teach contraception), birth control is "a way to have all the goodies and not pay the price," the "price" being pregnancy, of course. That's your punishment for being a big ol' whore.

The idea is that only sluts use contraception, because only sluts would have premarital sex. And when you have sex while you're married, you should be trying to pop out babies, so no birth control for you, either.

Basically, it's more of the same "sex is bad and shameful" crap. Sex isn't supposed to be fun, so they're not about to make it easy.

The bottom line? They don't care about our health. They don't care about increasing the number of abortions (which will inevitably happen if we don't have birth control access). All they care about is making sure that women aren't having sex, and that if we are, we're "punished." Period. But of course, most of them won't admit that.

I mean, even President Bush refuses to say whether he is for or against birth control. In 2005, former White House Press Secretary Scott McClellan refused to give Bush's stance on birth control. Since then, members of Congress have sent him four different letters asking him point blank whether he is for or against birth control—they've gotten no answer. Bush and the other anti-sexers know that if they let out how they *really* feel about contraception, too many people will catch on to their true agenda.

They know that the majority of Americans support birth control. Using contraception isn't some radical idea—it's pretty frigging normal. In fact, 99 percent of women will use birth control at one point in their lives.

That's why anti-choicers are so disturbing. Despite the fact that the majority of us think birth control is fine and dandy, lawmakers, powerful organizations, and even the president are creating new ways to keep birth control away from us every day.

Check this one out: At publication time, a lawmaker in Wisconsin, Representative Daniel LeMahieu, is close to ban-

> Many women who get abortions say that concern for their existing children is a key factor in their decision. That sounds like the opposite of "selfish" to me.

ning birth control from being distributed in any of that state's colleges. And again—it's all about The Sex or, in this case, fear of spring break. (Cue scary music.) LeMahieu got all bent out of shape when he saw an ad in a University of Wisconsin campus paper that recommended picking up some emergency contraception (EC) before heading out for spring break. Most would say a smart idea, no? Everyone knows that plenty of The Sexing goes on during spring break, and that in case a condom breaks it's good to have backup birth control. That's not exactly how LeMahieu saw it: "I am outraged that our public institutions are giving young college women the tools for having promiscuous sexual relations, whether on campus or thousands of miles away on spring break."[1]

Girls Gone Wild on Birth Control! Because who among us hasn't gotten a little wet in the panties when confronted with contraception? That plastic case is just so . . . sexy. Anyway, this ad started LeMahieu on his banning-birth-control crusade—it's just a matter of time before colleges in other states follow his lead.

Unfortunately, it's not just on college campuses that we can't get birth control. Women of all ages are being denied contraception at the one place you're supposed to be able to get it—the pharmacy. Imagine this: You take your monthly trip to the local pharmacy for your birth control pills. When you hand your prescription slip to the pharmacist, he randomly asks you if you're married or if you're using the pills to regulate your period. When you answer him (even though you'd like to smack him silly and tell him it's none of his business), you say that you use the pill for the reason most women do—to avoid getting pregnant—and no, you're not married. He tells you sorry, but he can't fill the prescription—he doesn't believe in premarital sex. Even when you inform him it doesn't really matter what *he* thinks, he still refuses. It gets so bad that you have to go find a police officer to escort you into the store and *force* him to give you your pills.

Sounds ridiculous (and fucking annoying), but this is what actually happened to college student Amanda Phiede in 2004 in Wisconsin—and that's just one woman's story.[2]

Pharmacists all over the country have been straight-up refusing to give women birth control, even though it's their job. And because of the introduction of something called "conscience clause laws," they're getting away with it. Thirteen states have introduced laws that would allow pharmacists,

nurses, and other healthcare professionals to refuse to dis-
tribute medication that goes against their moral, ethical, or
religious beliefs. So essentially, if a pharmacist thinks that
premarital sex is wrong, they don't have to give you your
pills. If contraception is against *their* religion, they don't have
to dispense *your* medication. I don't know about you, but
when I go to the pharmacy I just want my pills, not a lecture
about someone else's morals.

By the way, notice that pharmacists aren't refusing to
give men condoms or grilling them about their marital status.
The anti-sexers really only focus on women (since we're the
keepers of the all-powerful hymen, I guess).

I joke, but this is a huge deal. First it's birth control.
Next thing you know, nurses are refusing to treat gay
patients because homosexuality is against their religion. It's
scary shit.

And while some states are creating laws that would force
pharmacists and healthcare professionals to dispense contraception (you know, 'cause it's their job), it's not stopping
anti-sexers from stooping to new lows.

Dan Gransinger, a pharmacist at Kmart in Scottsdale,
Arizona, wrote a letter to the editor of *The Arizona Republic*
recommending that other pharmacists who have a problem
dispensing emergency contraception simply lie to their female customers:

❀ The pharmacist should just tell the patient that he
   is out of the medication and can order it, but it will

take a week to get here. The patient will be forced to go to another pharmacy because she has to take these medicines within seventy-two hours for them to be effective. Problem solved.[3]

Yes, he actually wrote this. You have to love how nonchalant he is about lying. As if it's no big deal . . . not to mention illegal.

We cannot let women be kept from their legal right to birth control! These new state laws that force pharmacists to do their jobs are a good first step, but with nutties like Gransinger around, it's clear that laws aren't enough. Find out about the birth control policies of your local pharmacist—make sure that women in your area aren't being denied their right to birth control.

The Morning After

There has been way too much confusion (put out there deliberately, mind you) about what exactly EC is. Is it the abortion pill? Is it birth control? Let's get this out of the way once and for all: Emergency contraception is *not* abortion.

And don't think for a second that you're uninformed or stupid because you didn't know this. The same folks who are trying to make sure that you don't have birth control are also trying to make sure that you are confused, and they are succeeding. A lot more people are against abortion than birth control. If they can make a form of birth control seem like a form of abortion, then they're closer to their goal of banning all birth control. They're doing it in baby steps.

Emergency contraception, also called the morning-after pill, is basically a large dose of birth control pills. It prevents you from getting pregnant; it *doesn't* end an existing pregnancy. EC will stop an egg from leaving the ovary, stop sperm from meeting the egg, or prevent a fertilized egg from implanting in your uterus. Despite the bullshit to the contrary, EC doesn't end pregnancy; it stops pregnancy from happening. Medical abortion—which you can find out about at the end of this chapter—is something completely different. Glad we have that out of the way.

In addition to the attempt to confuse EC with abortion, the other big lie being told about EC is that—like birth control—it will make you whorish. Especially if you're a teen girl. (Seems like anything will set us off on a fucking rampage, huh?) In fact, that's the main reason that EC isn't available without a prescription. The FDA stalled for years on giving EC over-the-counter status, using young women and their potential sluttiness as the excuse. They only (grudgingly) okayed it for over-the-counter sale in 2006, and even now it's only available to women over eighteen years old—leaving out the women who perhaps need it the

Male contraceptives are on the way! Two different kinds of pills (one hormonal, one not) and an IVD (similar to women's IUD) are being tested for release.

most: young women. I speak from personal experience when I tell you that EC is definitely not something that makes you particularly horny. When I was seventeen years old, I took it and felt sick to my stomach all day afterward.

In a 2006 investigation into the FDA's inappropriate lack of action on EC, a memo was found that shows just how insane the government has become over sex and young women. An FDA doctor said in the 2004 memo that one of the FDA heads, Dr. Janet Woodcock, expressed concern over EC and said that the FDA "could not anticipate or prevent extreme promiscuous behaviors, such as the medication taking on an 'urban legend' status that would lead adolescents to form sex-based cults centered around the use of [EC]."[4]

Teen sex cults? Sounds like a bad made-for-TV movie. I can see it now. Meredith Baxter Birney in *The Morning After*. "She thought her daughter was just 'spending time with friends.' Little did she know that Amy was just another teen dragged into the seedy world of teen sex cults."

But as ridiculous as this sounds, this *really* is the reason that women don't have access to a safe, legal form of contraception.

Even when the American Academy of Pediatrics released a policy statement in 2005 supporting over-the-counter access to EC (for adults *and* teens) and debunked the myth of EC causing promiscuity, the FDA continued to ignore the facts.

The FDA has also said that its stalling for over-the-counter status of EC really is a genuine concern for the health of teen girls, who might not take the drug properly. If that's the case, then why is it that a new diet pill—fat-blocking Orlistat—is on its way to over-the-counter approval? Experts voiced concerns over the possibility of teens abusing the drug and Orlistat's side effects, which include "fecal incontinence, gas, and oily discharge." Answer: They'd rather approve a diet pill that makes you shit your pants than a form of birth control. Politics are trumping science and safety. To this day, the agency refuses to admit that it won't approve EC simply because of anti-sex politics.

But perhaps the most distressing aspect of the EC madness is that women who need the drug most—rape victims— are being systematically denied it. Women who are sexually assaulted need easy access to EC perhaps more than anyone. These women are in an already-vulnerable position. But again, the anti-sexers don't have any sympathy for that kind of nonsense. (Rape? Pshaw.)

In 2005, the U.S. Department of Justice created the first-ever federal guidelines for treating sexual assault victims—but without *any* mention of EC, which is a standard precautionary measure after a rape. So basically, they created a national model for treating rape victims that states and local groups will look to when creating theirs. EC was deliberately left out of the guidelines and still isn't mentioned today—even though ninety-seven members of Congress urged the Justice Department to put it in there.

The truth is, even if EC were mentioned in the guidelines, there's no guarantee that rape survivors would be told about it. More and more reports are coming out that say hospitals are frequently remiss in their responsibility to tell rape victims about EC. Many Catholic hospitals even refuse to stock the drug, despite laws that tell them they must. Their excuse is that the woman can always go to another hospital if she *really* wants EC. Because clearly that's so easy.

For any of you who haven't been in an emergency room, that shit takes forever. Victims are in the hospital for hours. Imagine you've just been raped and you manage to gather the courage to get to a hospital. You wait for a couple of hours to be processed. Then, when a doctor finally sees you, you're told (if you're lucky enough to be told at all) that if you want to prevent getting pregnant by your rapist, you'll have to go to a different hospital and repeat the same process. It's beyond cruel. It's a despicable thing to ask of someone.

So now that I've depressed you sufficiently, what to do? Again, look into the policies at your local hospitals. Make sure that your friends, classmates, parents—everyone— knows about EC: that it's *not* abortion, that you have the right to get it at the pharmacy, and that it won't make you spontaneously burst into sex-crazed fits.

The Scarlet Letter

Obviously the Big A issue—abortion— is the most controversial one in repro rights, and maybe even in women's rights as a whole. Doctors and pro-choice volunteers have been killed over it. Women have died getting illegal abortions, and we're well on our way to having the right taken away. This shit is no joke.

> 77% of likely voters say that the government should stay out of a woman's personal and private decision about whether to have an abortion.

I'm not going to go into the whole moral argument over abortion, because honestly, it seems like a waste of time. Some people are going to believe what they want to believe, and that's that. All I can say is that I think there's nothing wrong with abortion, that the right to control our bodies is one of the most important there is, and that those who are seeking to end that right are concerned not about "life," but about control.

Abortion has become the new scarlet letter—the shameful secret that women are supposed to hide. Even though it's a *legal* medical procedure. Abortion means that you're selfish, that you're a slut, that you're a murderer. The truth is, one-third of American women will have an abortion in their lifetime. Are one-third of women morally deficient? Are they selfish sluts? Methinks not.

Women don't get abortions out of convenience or selfishness, though that's what the anti-choice movement would have you believe. They want you to think that abortion is an easy way out for "loose" women.

The truth? A study by the Guttmacher Institute shows that while women offer many reasons for choosing abortion, a huge reason is concern for children that they already have.

Get that—concern for children. According to Researcher
Lawrence B. Finer:

* There is a misconception that women take the decision to terminate a pregnancy lightly. . . . Women's
  primary reasons for making this difficult decision are
  based on a lack of resources in light of their current
  responsibilities. Typically, more than one reason
  drives the decision, and these reasons are frequently
  interrelated.[5]

Abortion is a moral choice. (Not to mention that pre-
venting unwanted pregnancies is a priority for pro-choicers—
we're the ones fighting for contraceptive choices and com-
monsense sex ed, not the folks who are anti-abortion.)

But no matter what the reason behind a woman's decision to have an abortion, it's none of anyone's business.
Try telling that to legislators! They're fully convinced that
they know what's best for women. Keep in mind most of
the people making these decisions are old white guys. Who
will never be pregnant. (Unless, of course, they're Arnold
Schwarzenegger in *Junior*, the weirdest movie of all time.)

Never mind that we're well on our way to Roe v. Wade
(the case that legalized abortion in 1973) being overturned;
there are so many restrictions in place right now, abortions
are near impossible to obtain anywhere. Eighty-seven percent
of counties in the United States have no abortion provider,
and even if they do, they're likely to be subject to any number
of ridiculous obstacles.

Mandatory waiting periods, for example, are one of the most common abortion restrictions. Basically, they make women who want an abortion wait a couple of days, supposedly to "think it over." Sounds harmless, but not only does it assume that a woman who wants an abortion hasn't *already* thought it over a great deal, it also puts a huge burden on poor women or women who live in rural areas. Most people can't take more than one day off work, and for women who live hundreds of miles away from the nearest abortion clinic, this is more than just a pain in the ass. But that's why the restriction is there; they're hoping women will be so put out that they won't bother coming back.

Eleven states are trying to ban abortion outright. South Dakota was already successful in doing so. Thankfully, after a massive pro-choice effort, the law was put on the 2006 ballot and voted down. But it was close. The big reason voters couldn't stand for it? South Dakotan lawmakers wanted to make it so even women who are raped or victims of incest couldn't get abortions. So, you might ask yourself, when is it okay to get an abortion? Listen to what South Dakota Senator Bill Napoli thinks (and try not to be too grossed out by his enthusiasm):

⊛ A real-life description to me would be a rape victim, brutally raped, savaged. The girl was a virgin. She was religious. She planned on saving her virginity until she was married. She was brutalized and raped, sodomized as bad as you can possibly make it, and is impregnated.[6]

Hear that, girls? If you want to get an abortion in South Dakota, you better make sure you've been raped *real* bad. And no hymen, no deal. As disgusting as this quote is (from a senator, no less), it pretty much sums up the anti-sex sentiment behind those who are fighting to end choice.

What kills me is that there's no shame in their game. Anti-sexers like Napoli will straight up say nasty-ass things but simultaneously claim they are looking out for women's best interest.

But hypocritical holier-than-thou attitudes aren't exactly new. The members of the anti-sex, anti-choice movement are supercareful about the language they use when talking about abortion, to make it seem like they are the "moral" ones. They use words like "life," "religious," and "family," but all the while they're thinking about virgins getting ass-raped. Lovely.

Lawmakers in Alabama, for example, introduced an abortion ban similar to the one in South Dakota; it would have no exception for rape and incest. Alabama Senator Hank Erwin said, "I thought if South Dakota can do it, Alabama ought to do it, because we are a family-friendly state."[7] Yeah,

Only one in five women knows about emergency contraception, and one-third of those women confuse EC with RU-486, the abortion pill.

'cause nothing says "family-friendly" like bullying rape and incest victims. Using sweet-as-pie language to describe forcing women to keep their rapists' babies—real classy.

The more extreme anti-choice folks who protest outside abortion clinics do the same kind of thing. For example, they'll say that they provide "sidewalk counseling," when what they're actually doing is screaming in women's faces that they're murderers as they walk into a clinic.

And it's not just the appropriation of "friendly" language, it's the fact that the anti-choice movement tells straight-up lies. And that so many people believe them.

Anti-Choice Lies

THE MYTH OF "PARTIAL-BIRTH" ABORTION

Repeat after me: There is no such thing as "partial-birth" abortion. You won't find it referenced in any medical journals or texts. It's a fictitious term created by anti-choicers in an attempt to ban *all* abortions. Anti-choicers will claim that the laws they're trying to pass will simply ban a late-term abortion procedure called intact dilation and extraction (D&E). This is a procedure that's hardly ever used, and when it is, it's generally because the fetus wouldn't be able to survive outside the womb, or because the mother's life is in danger. But the "partial-birth" abortion ban (which doesn't make an exception for the health of the woman) doesn't talk about this medical procedure. The legislation is so vaguely written that it could ban all abortions. Which, of course, is the point. You have to give the anti-choicers props, though—they strategically created this term, and they actually have people believing it.

ABORTION CAUSES BREAST CANCER

Abortion doesn't cause breast cancer. The National Cancer Institute, the American Cancer Society, and the American College of Obstetricians and Gynecologists have all said as much. Yet another very smart lie by the anti-choice, anti-sex sect. In reality, having a baby is actually more dangerous to your health than having an abortion. But that hasn't stopped anti-choicers from spreading misinformation and even trying to get legislation passed that would require telling women who want abortions that they're increasing their chance of getting breast cancer. Can you say "scare tactic"?

POST-ABORTION SYNDROME

Yet another fake term. It's not recognized by the scientific or medical communities. The idea is that women who have had abortions suffer mental trauma after the procedure. The truth of the "syndrome" is just more wordplay. It flips the script for the anti-choice movement. So many people see anti-choice activists as violent protesters that talking about a syndrome makes it seem like they care about women and their health. (If that were true, perhaps they wouldn't make shit up.) Again and again, studies have shown that women don't suffer mentally after an abortion. Naturally, different women will have different emotions after the procedure, but it seems to me that the stigmas attached to abortion (and having people scream that you're a murderer) would be contributing factors in all of this. In fact, the American Psychiatric Association says that "government restrictions on abortion are more likely to cause women lasting harm than the procedure itself."[8]

PREGNANCY CRISIS CENTERS

This is probably the worst of the anti-choice lies. "Pregnancy crisis centers" have been set up all over the country; in fact, there are more anti-choice crisis centers than health clinics that offer abortion. Basically, the centers tout themselves as women's health clinics and lead women to believe that they offer abortion and birth control services. Of course, they don't. Essentially, they're there to intimidate or trick women into remaining pregnant. They have two strategies to do this. Sometimes they tell women that they don't have any more appointments and she should call back. They continue to put her off—maybe even schedule an abortion and then cancel—until she is too far along in the pregnancy to have a legal abortion. Other anti-choice crisis centers will simply bully women. Writer/feminist blogger Amanda Marcotte tells one girl's story:

> ❉ According to a recent Planned Parenthood email, a seventeen-year-old girl mistakenly walked into a crisis pregnancy center thinking it was Planned Parenthood, which was next door. The group took down the girl's confidential personal information

and told her to come back for her appointment, which they said would be in their "other office" (the real Planned Parenthood office nearby).

When she showed up for her nonexistent appointment, she was met by the police, who had been erroneously tipped that a minor was being forced to abort. The crisis pregnancy center staff followed up this harassment by staking out the girl's house, phoning her father at work, and even talking to her classmates about her pregnancy, urging them to harass her.[9]

Oh, and by the way—your taxes pay for these places. Sit on that one for a while.

WE'RE PROTECTING THE CHILDREN!

Another big fat lie is that anti-choicers are just trying to protect children from scary child molesters and abortionists. The biggest proponent of this bullshittery is former Kansas Attorney General Phill Kline, who, until 2006, was on a one-man crusade to make sure that teens didn't screw—I mean, are protected.

While in office (he was voted out in 2006), Kline tried to get the medical records of more than ninety women who had abortions. But medical records are private, you say? Not his problem. Kline claimed he was looking for evidence of statutory rape, to see if any of the women who had abortions were under sixteen. Never mind that Kline ignored a case in which a thirteen-year-old in his state got knocked up and married a twenty-two-year-old. It's simply anti-sex nonsense and privacy invasion shrouded in rhetoric about protecting kids. Case in point: Kline also tried to get a law passed requiring healthcare professionals to report (as in, to the police) *any sexual activity* between people under sixteen years old. Even if both hooker-uppers are underage. Even if they don't have sex. (I love the idea of getting reported for going to second base. Hysterical.)

But this kind of nonsense is par for the course when it comes to teens and abortion rights.

Mother may I . . . ?

There isn't anything quite as annoying to me as parental consent and notification laws for abortion. Not only do these laws presuppose that young women aren't capable of making decisions for themselves about their own bodies, but they also assume that kids *won't* tell their parents—which just isn't true.

Thirty-four states have some sort of parental involvement law. Some states require that parents be notified; others say you actually need a written note from your parents okaying the procedure. Arizona even requires that young women have a notarized written note! Next you'll have to jump through flaming hoops while balancing a spoon on your nose or some shit.

The logic behind the laws is that parents should be involved in their kids' lives. Okay, I can understand that. But the truth is, most teens *do* tell their parents if they're pregnant. And the ones who don't generally have a pretty good reason not to—like incest or abuse. These laws don't take that into consideration.

Imagine that a teen girl gets raped by her father and becomes pregnant. She's seriously supposed to go to *him* to get permission for an abortion?! Now, most states do have some sort of judicial bypass, which means you can go in front of a judge and explain why you can't tell your parents about the pregnancy. This is just crap. If you're being abused at home, you know that if you tell a judge, officials are going to have to intervene somehow. You're risking your whole world being turned upside down. Besides, the idea of going in front of a judge is terrifying to anyone—let alone a scared, pregnant, abused teen!

As scary as it is, some teens don't even have that option. Republican Senator Chris Buttars of Utah recently tried to defend a bill that would get rid of the judicial-bypass option— even for victims of incest. But you have to love that he didn't even deny his real motives. Senator Buttars said, "Abortion isn't about women's rights. The rights they had were when they made the decision to have sex. . . . This is the consequence. The consequence is they should have to talk to their parents."[10] Even if your parent is the one who got you pregnant. Love that logic. (The consequence of having the last name Buttars is apparently being a huge asshole. Appropriate.)

The bottom line is, these laws are not about keeping teen girls safe. They're about controlling them. Apparently we're too naive to decide what to do with our own bodies without permission from a parent or husband. Yeah, you heard right: husband. A lot of these parental involvement laws are only enforceable if the teen is unmarried. So if you're a married teenager, you can get an abortion. Somehow a sixteen-year-old with a husband is better able to decide if she wants a child?

Once again, just more slut-punishing. If you're married, it means you're a good girl. Your prize for not having unmarried sex? Control of your body. You're single and pregnant? Well, then someone else has to make the decision for you. Sucks for you, slut.

These gross consent laws are starting to trickle down into birth control, too. Like I mentioned before, the irrational fear of *Girls Gone Wild* has made for quite a difficult time for young women. Some states even require teens to get

A 2006 report showed that 87% of "pregnancy crisis" centers—which have received more than $30 million in federal funding—provided false or misleading information about abortion.

a written note from their parents just to get birth control. My parents were cool with my being on birth control when I was younger, but I doubt they wanted to know the details. I mean, imagine knowing the intimate details of your mom's diaphragm. Ew.

Other states just defy logic. In New York, Governor George Pataki refused to make EC available over the counter for fear that teenage girls would have access to the drug. The kicker? Teenage girls can get abortions in New York without parental notification or consent. So they're allowed to end a pregnancy, but not prevent one. Yeah, I know.

At the end of the day, though, the entire basis for consent laws doesn't make sense. We're not old enough to decide if we *don't* want a baby, but we are old enough to have one?

Of course, if we're not straight and white—it's a different story.

Mommie Dearest

You would think, given how gung ho anti-sexers seem to be about making sure you have babies, that it would be easy for everyone. But slow down, sister. Not everyone is "appropriate" for child rearing under the narrow guidelines of the chastity club.

LESBIANS NEED NOT APPLY

In one of the cruelest moves ever, the anti-sex, anti-gay crowd (they tend to go hand in hand) is trying to keep anyone who isn't straight or married from being parents. Both Indiana and Virginia have been trying to pass laws that would keep unmarried women from using "reproductive technology," like artificial insemination or fertility treatments. While the legislation would affect all unmarried women, it was written specifically with lesbians in mind.

They're the ones who the lawmakers figured are more likely not to be married (because it's illegal) and to be seeking help getting pregnant.

In fact, the proposed law in Virginia made it pretty clear—if you're not having heterosexual (married) sex, you can't have a kid:

❋ No individual licensed by a health regulatory board shall assist with or perform any intervening medical technology, whether in vivo or in vitro, *for or on an unmarried woman, that completely or partially replaces sexual intercourse as the means of conception*, including, but not limited to, artificial insemination by donor, cryopreservation of gametes and embryos, in vitro fertilization, embryo transfer, gamete intrafallopian tube transfer, and low tubal ovum transfer.[11] [Emphasis added.]

So basically: No dick, no deal.

Forced Birth Control?

Given how hard the anti-sexers are trying to keep birth control away from so many young women, the idea of forcing birth control on someone seems a little wacky. But of course, these are the teen-sex-cult people we're talking about.

When women started fighting for reproductive rights back in the '60s and '70s, the most attention was paid to the battle for birth control and abortion rights. But what went unnoticed by many—and still is largely ignored to this day—

was the fight to stop women from being sterilized. As in no more kids, ever.

Coercive sterilization and forced long-term birth control (like Depo or IUDs) were pushed on women fairly often back then. But because this was happening mostly to poor women and women of color, it didn't garner national attention.

Women who were on welfare were misled into thinking they wouldn't receive their benefits if they didn't go along with the sterilization. One story stood out among the hundreds that went unreported. In the '60s, three African American sisters—sixteen, fourteen, and twelve years old—were subjected to forced sterilizations without their consent. By the government. While the Relf family was being directed to a housing project, a congressional program recommended that the girls take advantage of family planning services. One of the daughters was given an IUD; the other two were sterilized. Their mother—who was illiterate—was told to sign a form that said the girls were just being given "some shots."[12] Beyond horrifying.

Unfortunately, initiatives like that aren't a thing of the past. Coercive sterilization and long-term birth control are still being pushed—under the guise of helping women. Back when I was interning at *Ms.* magazine, I heard about an organization called CRACK (Children Requiring a Caring Kommunity) that was absolutely terrifying. It's since changed its name to Project Prevention (much friendlier sounding), but its tactics are still the same. The organization pays female drug addicts in exchange for getting long-term birth control and surgical sterilization. Outside of how disgusting that is on its face—let's just sterilize women, not get them treatment—the group's blatant racist and classist tactics make it beyond reprehensible.

These women, after all, aren't just any drug addicts. The project puts up billboards in poor black neighborhoods that say things like: ADDICTED TO DRUGS? WANT $200? One of its other strategies is to approach women in soup kitchens. I wonder how many billboards went up in rich white areas where women are snorting coke at their kid's birthday party or popping Xanax like Tic Tacs.

Barbara Harris, the organization's founder, has compared her clients to animals: "We don't allow dogs to breed. We spay them. We neuter them. We try to keep them from having unwanted puppies, and yet these women are literally having litters of children."[13]

"These women," huh?

Wyndi Anderson at National Advocates for Pregnant Women says that CRACK (I'm sorry, I refuse to call it Project Prevention) relies on the same economic arguments to support its program as were used to justify eugenics sterilization in the United States and Nazi Germany. She points out that there are real solutions to help women:

❀ There are things we can do to help women and families. Make sure that when a woman asks for help she can get it. Too often women and other people seeking help for addictions are put on waiting lists, told to come back later, given a referral to a program that will not in fact take them, or told that they are ineligible because they do not have the right kind of insurance. Make sure that women with drug problems are treated the same as other patients.[14]

But it's so much easier to do some tube-tying!

The repro rights movement is probably the most well-known women's issue around, but this aspect of it is hardly ever talked about. Don't forget that repro rights and health are about a lot more than abortion and birth control.

So Are We Totally Screwed?

So, I know it sounds bleak. And in a big way, it is.

The Supreme Court is mostly anti-choice—there's a good chance Roe will be reversed. And the prevailing anti-sex attitude that's behind all of the rollbacks on repro rights isn't showing any signs of going away.

I don't mean to be a downer, but best to be honest, right?

All isn't lost, though. Women are fighting like crazy to make sure that we hold on to the rights we have and get back the ones we've lost. The pro-choice effort in South Dakota was an amazing example of this. Women collected more than 38,000 signatures (more than twice the number needed) to put the issue on the ballot. Then, even in the face of the anti-choice community putting out straight-up lies about the law (saying there was a rape and incest exception), they went out, door to door, and made sure the truth was being told. And

it paid off. Young women across the country are having parties, events, and fundraisers to raise awareness about repro
rights and take action. A group in Brooklyn, for example, is
having a "Burlesque for Choice" party. Fun. And remember
creepy Senator Bill Napoli, who said only super-sodomized
virgins should be able to have abortions? A female comic did
a strip making fun of him and included his home and office
numbers. Women from all over the country gave Mr. Sodomy
a call and told him exactly what they thought of him.

Young women are the ones who are being royally screwed
by all this, but we're also the ones taking innovative action.
I'll sometimes hear that women my age or younger "don't
know how good they have it," or that we take our rights for
granted. I call bullshit. We know what the stakes are, and
we're doing what's necessary. The only question is—what
will you do?

I'm opting in

6

MATERIAL WORLD

Guess what? The pay gap still exists! (I'm sure you're shocked.) The good news is that we've made some progress. In 2009, President Obama signed the Lily Ledbetter Fair Pay Act, which makes it easier for women to sue for discrimination over unequal pay. Culturally, the conversation about women and work has gained traction as well. Thanks to women like Sheryl Sandberg—the COO of Facebook—and Ann-Marie Slaughter, whose piece on "having it all" (however flawed) caused waves—women and work/life issues are hot topics right now. The problem, however, is that the discourse around women's professional lives—how much they're paid, ambition, how they "juggle" children and work—is very much still centered on the most privileged among us. But feminists are looking to change that. Through work like that being done by the Domestic Workers Alliance, we can focus on the intersection of race, class, work, and gender—94 percent of domestic workers are women and they earn 23 percent less than state minimum wage. Until the focus is shifted to the most marginalized in work and economic equality issues, we're going to continue to talk in circles.

Women work. We have to. So why is it that we're still being told that our "natural" place is at home? Sure, women aren't getting the old 1950s barefoot-and-pregnant crap— but there's still a strong movement that wants us to backtrack our asses to the kitchen, despite the reality of women working. Regardless of the retro messages (be they from the media, government, or otherwise), women are working in force. Still, we're 40 percent more likely to be poor, earn significantly less than men—and we continue to work that second shift—and do the bulk of the cooking, cleaning, and childcare! So all is definitely not well.

Now, plenty of people—mostly old white guys with high-paying jobs—are arguing that this is all going on because of women's choices. We *want* to spend more time at home, so it's only *natural* that we make less and climb the ranks slower. My ass. The vast majority of American women can't afford not to work—there's no choice about it. And these folks who argue that women aren't making money because we don't *want* to are the same ones who think that women belong in the home: They're the leaders from conservative organizations, popular columnists, and even decision-makers in the government. Traditional ideas about women working are more common than you'd think, and there's a movement of powerful people out there making sure that their messages are getting across—to you.

It's young women who are most affected by this; we're the ones starting our careers and maybe even families (married or not). Yet we're still being fed the same drivel that our mothers and grandmothers were—in revamped language, of course. Ideas about women not wanting to work are being pushed under the rhetoric of "choice" (I know, it's *our* word!): Women choose to make less, women choose to stay home, women choose not to work as hard. It remains to be seen how many of us will actually fall for this nonsense, but the prevalence of the message is disturbing enough. And when we *do* have children, the same people who were pushing us to be happy homemakers are nowhere to be seen.

The thing that worries me? Of all the issues that young women talk about and get excited about, this seems to be at the bottom of the list. And that seems strange. The things that will potentially affect us the most in life—work, family, money—are the things we discuss the least. That needs to change.

The Not So Fun Truth about Women Working

Most women work outside of the home—and have been for some time. So you would think that working life for the gals would be fine by now. Or at least a lot better. Unfortunately, not so much. Some of the same obstacles that existed decades ago are still around in force. Whether it's pay inequity, harassment, discrimination, or outright lies about the very existence of working women—we're still facing plenty of hurdles.

WHO NEEDS A DOLLAR WHEN YOU HAVE SEVENTY-SIX CENTS?

It's pretty unbelievable, but women are still earning significantly less than men in the workplace—and we haven't made that much headway over the years. The Equal Pay Act was signed in 1963, when women were making about 60 percent of what men did. By 1990, that number went up to 70 percent. Now? It's a measly 76 percent. Not much of an improvement for more than forty years of so-called progress. Fuckers.

What really pisses me off about the wage gap, though, is that some people are saying it doesn't exist. Never mind that these statistics come from the government. Whether it's from the media, conservative pundits, or even the government, their argument is full of crap but scarily prevalent. The common line is that women make less because we take time off to care for kids and family members. My favorite anti-feminist organization, the Independent Women's Forum (IWF), has actually made a career out of making this claim.

Former IWF President Nancy Pfotenhauer has said, "Women often make different choices than men. . . . Many women are willing to trade more money for more flexibility. [They] choose jobs that offer greater flexibility so that they can spend more time with their families. . . . This is a choice that women should be able to make."[1] Another conservative, Warren Farrell, makes his living trying to dispute the

The Supreme Court ruled in 2005 that employees can sue when businesses retaliate against them for making sexual harassment claims.

wage gap. Even worse, he does it in a way that makes it seem like he's *helping* women. He wrote a book called *Why Men Earn More: The Startling Truth Behind the Pay Gap—and What Women Can Do About It*. Yeah, right. Farrell says that the wage gap exists because of the choices women make—because they stay at home with their kids or because they cut back to part-time, for example. The problem with arguments like the IWF's and Farrell's? They're total bullshit. The government stat reporting that women make only seventy-six cents to a man's dollar comes from data that looks at women and men who work full-time. It doesn't include women who took time off or who worked part-time. So there.

Despite the fact that these folks are clearly talking out of their asses, they're getting heard. Not only do reputable news sources quote them constantly, but they have pull with government leaders as well.

In fact, in 2004 the Bureau of Labor Statistics (BLS) decided that reporting on women's wages wasn't a priority anymore—so they decided to stop. A sneaky move if there ever was one; if the government doesn't collect data about women's earnings, then we won't know how they compare to men's. So no more wage-gap talk from those annoying feminists. Thankfully, in 2005, the Senate passed an amendment that required the BLS to continue collecting info on women's pay.[2] But it was a close call.

How to fix the wage gap is a whole other story. Discrimination is widespread, so it's no easy task. One study out of the University of North Carolina says—and this makes sense to me—that having more women in high-ranking positions can narrow the pay gap.[3] The study reported that American women earn more if women in their company are in senior-level positions; the idea being that women will help other women out. So climb the ranks, gals! We need you there. If only the way to the top weren't littered with oh-so-fun hurdles like sex discrimination.

GLASS-CEILING MADNESS

Like the wage gap, the glass ceiling is still alive and kicking. Women aren't in senior positions in the same numbers as men, and they face more obstacles along the way. The glass ceiling (a term started in the '80s to describe the "invisible" barriers that stop women from advancing in the workplace) may be even more relevant than in years past, because now, similar to what we're hearing about the wage gap, people try to argue that it doesn't exist.

The truth is, it's still pretty hard for women at work. I'll spare you the stats (you can get those at the end of the chapter), but let's just say women in top positions at corporations are few and far between. Especially when it comes to women of color.

But I thought we've come a long way, baby?! While there's no doubt that working life for women is better than it once was, sometimes it seems that not a whole lot has changed.

In the 1960s, the National Organization for Women (NOW) fought for women flight attendants; they were routinely fired for getting pregnant or for being over age thirty-five. The organization also brought attention to help-wanted ads that were separated out by gender. Crazy, right? Antiquated sexism of the past? I wish.

In 2004, Viacom sent out an email about a job opening in the government relations department reading, "We need to hire a junior lobbyist/PAC manager. Attached is a job description. Salary is $85–90K. Must be a male with Republican stripes."[4] In 2005, Virgin Airlines was sued for hiring women based on their looks and age.[5] And these are just two examples. (Glad to see we've come so far.)

I'm not trying to be a downer, but trying to pretend that we're all good now just means we're ignoring the discrimination that still happens—something we can't afford to do.

So now that we're all up to speed, here are some common barriers that keep women in lower job ranks:

SEX DISCRIMINATION

It's illegal to discriminate against someone because of their sex (or race, color, national organization, or religion, for that matter), but it still happens all the time. The Federal Glass Ceiling Commission found that one of the reasons for discrimination is a "difference" barrier that "manifests through

conscious and unconscious stereotyping and bias."[6] So basically, the people who do the hiring like hiring people who
look like them. And if it's a white guy doing the hiring . . .
well, you see where I'm going. Sex discrimination also relates
to pay, promotions, and general treatment at work. One of
the biggest sex discrimination cases to date is a class action
suit against Wal-Mart. The corporate giant has been accused
of systematically denying women promotions and paying
them less. In fact, women make up more than 70 percent of
the company's hourly workforce but less than a third of its
management.[7]

SEXUAL HARASSMENT

The U.S. Equal Employment Opportunity Commission defines sexual harassment as "unwelcome sexual advances,
requests for sexual favors, and other verbal or physical
conduct of a sexual nature" that affects a person's ability
to do his or her job or creates "an intimidating, hostile, or
offensive work environment."[8] So ass-grabbing is definitely
out. I joke, but this is serious stuff. Work can be torture for
women who are being sexually harassed. And for women
who need their jobs to survive (which is most of us), this is
an awful situation. Just a couple of examples: A woman in
California was spanked—yes, spanked—in front of cowork-
ers.[9] And an August 2006 report even showed that a large
number of women who try to join the military are abused
and harassed by their recruiters.[10] Sweet, huh?

WORK/LIFE BALANCE

Plenty of people will become parents while they're working—but it's women who take the brunt of discrimination against parents and soon-to-be-parents. Though it's illegal, employers will routinely not hire young women they think might get pregnant in the near future. Bad for business, you know, 'cause you'll have to take time off to give birth and such. Beyond that, parenting can take a real toll on a career. Statistics show that mothers earn less and less with each child they have. Welcome to the Mommy Wage Gap. For the first kid a woman has, the wage difference between her salary and a non-mommy's is 2 to 10 percent less. For the second kid, the gap grows to 4 to 16 percent less. And the reasons why moms get paid less aren't what you think. A Cornell University study showed that with equal resumes, job experience, and education, not only were women with children 44 percent less likely to be hired than women without children, but when they were offered a position, their starting annual salary was $11,000 lower on average.[11] So as Kristin Rowe-Finkbeiner, coauthor of *The Motherhood Manifesto*, said in an interview with Feministing, "This is an actual bias

Men outnumber women six to one in top corporate jobs.

up front against mothers—not because of something moms are doing wrong, but because with equal circumstances, the bias is there."[12] The Mommy Wage Gap isn't there because moms take more time off, or because they don't work as hard. You do the math.

MEDIA LIES: OPT OUT, MY ASS

While the media madness surrounding women and work isn't something that directly affects women's day-to-day work lives, it's something I have to mention because it affects how we all see work and women's roles.

The "women's choices" line of reasoning has been around for a while, but it's made a hardcore comeback in the media these last few years. The worst one I've heard yet? Lisa Belkin, a writer for *The New York Times,* wrote an article on women "opting out" of work in order to stay at home with the kiddies.[13] Her subtitle: "Why don't women run the world? Maybe it's because they don't want to."

As horrible a tagline as that was, boy, did it cause a stir. That one frigging article from 2003 has been reborn a million times over in the media. And it's wrong every time. Belkin's original piece argued that all these highly educated women were dropping out of the workforce to take care of their kids and be housewives because they found it more enjoyable. The problem? Belkin's theory was based on the idea that *all* the women in America are like the Harvard MBA–holding, rich-ass white women she interviewed. Yeah, not so much. Most women don't have the financial ability to just decide not to work. Not to mention that just because a handful of elite women are doing something doesn't make it a social trend. But since the Belkin piece ran, countless similar articles have followed, citing the same "opt out" nonsense. While a couple of articles may not seem like a big deal, the fact is, they put out the false notion of a "trend." And duh, trends are trendy. Telling young women that the cool new shit is to stay at home (and this, of course, entails having a rich hubby) is not exactly the best message in the world.

The truth? Women aren't opting out. We can't! Even those who do have the financial options aren't dropping out of the workforce. The Center for Economic Policy and Research put out a paper this year titled "Are Women Opting Out?"[14] The answer was a resounding "hells no." The paper noted that "the early 2000s recession led to sustained job losses for all women—those with and without children at home," and "between 2000 and 2004, thirtysomething mothers with advanced degrees saw no statistically significant change in the effect of children on their labor force participation rates."[15] In fact, the women who did leave the workforce because of childcare responsibilities often did so because of the Mommy Wage Gap!

This isn't to say that women aren't ever making the decision to stay home and raise families—they are. But given the economy and a host of other factors, it's just not as common as some people would like you to think. And when women *do* stay home, they have a whole new set of worries.

The Unloved/Unpaid Labor

Unfortunately, but not exactly shockingly, women do the majority of the work in the household. You know, all the fun stuff like cleaning toilets and doing laundry. And this isn't just women who don't have jobs outside the home—it's all married women. A recent Department of Labor study showed that women spend twice as much time as men on household chores and taking care of kids. That's in addition to their paying jobs. Fun, huh? In fact, in July 2006 *The New York Times* reported that unemployed men do less work around the house than women who have full-time jobs.[16] Yeah, that sounds fair.

When it comes to moms who don't work outside the home, their work (shockingly) is ridiculously underappreciated. A recent study by Salary.com actually showed that if a full-time stay-at-home mom was paid for all of the work she does, she'd be getting $134,121 a year.[17] Now that's some money.

The stay-at-home-mom stuff is talked about a lot in feminist circles—especially since all this "opt out" nonsense started. Some women say that the whole idea behind femi-

A 2006 report says that 71.8% of Yale women (who supposedly wanted to opt out?) would take less than one year off work after their children are born.

nism is that we exercise our choices—and that if some women want to stay at home rather than work, we should respect that. Others, like author Linda Hirshman, say that not working is just a bad idea all around. Hirshman makes the case in her book *Get to Work: A Manifesto for Women of the World* that women are selling themselves short if they "opt out," and that being engaged in the world at large—rather than just the one at home—is necessary.[18] She especially hates the old saying that moms are "doing the most important job" in the world by raising kids:

> ❖ If, in fact, it were the most important thing a human being could do, then why are no men doing it? They'd rather make war, make foreign policy, invent nuclear weapons, decode DNA, paint *The Last Supper,* put the dome on St. Peter's Cathedral; they'd prefer to do all those things that are much less important than raising babies?[19]

You have to admit she has a point. But don't get your panties in a bunch; Hirshman is being deliberately controversial in order to get the conversation started. Because I have to agree that once we start talking about how wonderful it is that smart gals with PhDs are cleaning up poopie all day, something is a little off.

To Kid or Not to Kid

So let's say you want to go the mommy route. Considering all the social and political forces telling you that all women are

good for is popping out babies, you would think that those same forces would make taking care of those kids easier. Guess again. Not only is the United States one of only two industrialized nations that doesn't provide paid leave for new parents, Americans are sometimes paying up to 50 percent of their salary for childcare.[20] That is some ridiculous shit.

According to childcare advocacy project The Family Initiative, 63 percent of all kids under six years old in the United States receive some kind of childcare or education from someone other than their parent.[21] The group did a study on the average yearly cost to provide a one-year-old with childcare: It ranged from more than $12,000 in Boston to more than $3,000 in Knoxville. That's a lot of money for anyone, but for families and parents who are lower income, that's an incredible burden. The study also found that 60 percent of low-income families (who earn less than $1,200 a month) pay out 37 percent of their income toward childcare.[22] Nuts.

The kicker? The same politicians who are voting against legislation to ease childcare costs for poor parents are scamming money for their own kids! A *Washington Post* editorial pointed out that some members of Congress are using campaign funds to pay for their childcare. Republican Representative John T. Doolittle from California, for example, who received the lowest possible score from the Children's Defense Fund for his votes on funding for childcare, Head Start, and after-school programs, had his campaign reelection committee and his leadership political action committee pay more than $5,000 in childcare costs for his daughter.[23] And you can bet he's not the only one.

All I'm saying is that for a government that seems to want us to have babies, they're sure unhelpful once the kids are *outside* the uterus. Where are our government-funded preschools? Other countries have them. Shit, if they want us to be moms so badly, the least they could do is give us a little incentive.

So seriously, when we think about issues like reproductive rights, we should be thinking childcare, too! It's easy to get caught up in fights like violence against women and repro rights because they're so in your face. But something like childcare has a huge and lasting effect on women's lives; it's just not as evident.

I'm all for having babies, but just keep this in mind: Research shows that for every year a woman in her twenties waits to have children, her lifetime earnings increase by 10 percent. Just saying.

Money

FEMINIZATION OF POVERTY

It's pretty messed up, but women are more likely to be poor in a trend some feminists call the "feminization of poverty." Basically, this means women are more likely to have jobs that pay less, like in the service industry (think waitress, teacher, secretary). The question a lot of feminists ask is: Are these jobs low-paying because they're jobs associated with women? Like, if droves of men wanted to be teachers, would teaching all of a sudden become a high-paying profession? Just something to think about.

IN THE POOR HOUSE? GET A MAN.

This seeming obsession with women being happy little wifeys goes beyond the media and pop culture. It's actually keeping women poor. The powers that be would actually rather that women were poor than unmarried. Serious.

American women are 40 percent more likely than men to be poor. In fact, 90 percent of welfare recipients are women. But instead of spending money on things like education and job-training programs, the government is pouring all sorts of cash into—get this—marriage-promotion programs.

In March 2006, President Bush committed $100 million a year for the next five years to a "Healthy Marriage Initiative," as part of a welfare bill. This money, which would have been used for education, childcare, and job training, is now allocated to religious-based programs that tell women that getting married is the best way out of poverty. (Who needs a job when you have a man?!)

Of course, the gov folks swear up and down that the programs are just common sense. Wade Horn, assistant secretary for children and families at the U.S. Department of Health and Human Services, says that marriage promotion helps "couples who choose marriage for themselves gain greater access, on a voluntary basis, to services where they can develop the skills and knowledge necessary to form and sustain a healthy marriage."[24]

But what they really mean when they say a "healthy" marriage is a "traditional" one (and a straight one, of course). And for the guys in power now, a traditional marriage is one in which women don't work.

Just check out what these programs *actually* do. In 2004, one of the first marriage-promotion programs was charged with sex discrimination. The Family Formation and Development Project in Allentown, Pennsylvania, a twelve-week marriage education course for unmarried couples with children, offered employment services as part of the program—but only to men.[25] Nice, huh? Another program, the biblically based Marriage Savers, makes the case for marriage using logic that sounds like it came from a 1950s home ec textbook: "The married man won't go to work hungover, exhausted, or tardy because of fewer bachelor habits, and because he eats better and sees the doctor sooner, thanks to his wife. She is also a good adviser on career decisions, and relieves him of chores, so he can do a better job."[26]

You got that, gals? Men should be the breadwinners, and women should be dependent on them. The government wants happy housewives. More than they want financially secure women.

Something kind of funny: When I was working with NOW Legal Defense and Education Fund, a women's legal rights organization, a lot of the work I did concerned women working in nontraditional jobs—like construction work, mechanics, and firefighting. These kinds of jobs have proven to be awesome ways for low-income women and women with-

> A study out of the U.K. says that mothers who work outside the home have better health than stay-at-home moms.

out a college education to make more money. The hours are flexible (a must for women with children), the money is great, and there's amazing potential for career growth.

And while any job training is preferable to pushing tired sexist stereotypes about poverty and marriage, non-traditional jobs are much better paying than "pink collar" professions (again, service industry stuff). In 1996, for example, the average weekly earnings for cashiers, waitresses, and hairdressers ranged from $200 to $300, whereas women rail workers and women electricians earned $700 and $800, respectively.[27] But even though jobs like these have proven to be a good way to get women out of poverty, you won't see the government funding any nontraditional employment programs—at least not significantly. Because god forbid a woman is in a hard hat with cash in her pocket, rather than at home, broke.

Making the Connections

I know this seems all over the place: money, kids, work. And there's a lot more where that came from that I didn't get into—god knows there's a ton of stuff to cover. But the point

I want to make is that all of these things are interrelated—in a scary way.

A great example: As I was finishing this chapter, *Forbes* magazine—supposedly a reputable business publication— put out an article called "Don't Marry Career Women."[28] Yeah, I know.

The author, Michael Noer (who, incidentally, also wrote an article comparing the economic viability of wives versus hookers), says that if you marry a woman with a career, you're in for a lifetime of pain. He cites all the bullshit articles and studies I've talked about, and argues that if a man marries a woman who works, he's in for all kinds of problems: She'll cheat; divorce is more likely; the couple is less likely to have kids and more likely to have a dirty house(!). And the list goes on and on.

Though *Forbes* eventually apologized for the article, this kind of nonsense is the perfect example of just how common these types of arguments are becoming. The thing to remember about all of this—the media messages, the stats, everything—is that it's part of a larger agenda to reinforce traditional gender roles. And it's true that not everyone wants to reclaim traditional gender roles, but a lot of the people in power do. (And I'm betting they read *Forbes*, natch.) And the folks who are trying to convince you that it's cool to stay home and not work are the same ones who are screwing women over when it comes to the wage gap, childcare, and poverty. So don't fall for their shit.

The truth? Discrimination still exists in the workplace, there's a significant pay gap between men and women, women are *not* choosing to stay at home, and we're facing a crisis when it comes to women and poverty.

But of course, instead of focusing on real issues of discrimination and work/life conflicts, society is busy feeding women distractions so that we don't focus on them, either.

I pay my
own way

MY BIG FAT UNNECESSARY WEDDING
AND OTHER DATING DISEASES

When *FFF* came out, I had just met the guy who would eventually become my husband—we married in 2009. One of the funnier things about getting hitched—especially considering this chapter—was how strongly people seemed to feel about a feminist getting married. Some of the concern was well-founded and I shared it. I struggled with how I could get married when it's a right that's not afforded to everyone. I'm happy to say support for same-sex marriage has increased over the years and more states have legalized marriage equality, but we're still not there. Some of the criticism I ran into was about the wedding itself—is there such a thing as a feminist wedding in the face of the intense wedding industrial complex? I'm not sure I know the answer for sure, but this is how we handled it. We wanted to make the wedding representative of the institution we'd like marriage to be. I didn't wear a white dress, I had both parents walk me down the aisle (as did he), and I kept my last name. We talked about marriage equality in our vows and let our guests know we had donated money to organizations supporting marriage equality. Does any of this change the fact that marriage is a historically sexist institution or make it okay that millions of people are denied the right to be married? Of course not. But it made our wedding one that reimagined what marriage as an institution *should* be about: love, equal partnership, and community. (And seriously, for some of the more conservative relatives, hearing these sort of things at a wedding absolutely made an impact.) We need to change marriage culturally and politically, but also rethink what it means to us personally.

There's something terrifying about the way relationship fever takes over women, or at least about how it's expected to take us over. We're expected to go from boy crazy when we're little (remember, lesbians don't exist) to bridezillas as adults. Landing a man is assumed to be our main goal in life, trumping any other desires. And while a little romance never hurt anybody, the idea that women are supposed to be obsessively focused on all things love- and relationship-oriented serves a strategic, anti-feminist purpose. Because if all we're thinking about is how to get a guy, then maybe we won't pay such close attention to the fact that we're getting paid less at work or having our reproductive rights stripped away.

Now you're saying to yourself, *See, I knew feminists were just a bunch of anti-male killjoys!* Slow your roll. This isn't a diatribe against all things romantic. Shit, I'm as much a sucker for flowers as the next girl. Everyone likes being in love. Unless, of course, your object of desire is an asshole or doesn't like you back—but that's a problem for another book. The issue isn't love and sex. It's the expectation that this is *all* women should care about. And don't even try to tell me that that's not the case. What is the focus of pretty much *all* women's magazines? TV shows? According to pop culture, women are either searching for a man, with a man, or getting over one.

Perhaps the most disturbing part of all the love mania that we're subjected to is that it's increasingly consumer based. If you're not buying something, you're not in love. Forget romantic connections and chemistry—it's about the gifts, the dates, the wedding dress, the ring. More and more, young women are being taught that you can measure love in dollars. And that's dangerous for men *and* women.

I think that romantic relationships or life partnerships are truly important parts of our lives—but they're not the only part. Women are being taught that all we're worth is what guys think of us. This screws up younger women particularly, because that indoctrination starts early and takes a while to get rid of (if you ever do). When you learn from an early age that the best a girl can hope for is to be desired by boys, you're going to do everything you can to make sure that you are desired. Period.

A whopping $72 billion per year is spent on weddings.

So as lovely as romance can be, we have to make sure that we're not falling into the trap of making our entire life about searching for an unrealistic notion of happiness. While falling in love is fun, it's not everything, and it's not the antidote to an unfulfilled life, despite what Reese Witherspoon movies may tell you.

Even the most feminist of us (ahem) can get carried away. After my long-term college relationship ended (hi, Mike!), I was eager to get into the dating world. I went on a bit of a trampage (sorry, Mike). I was doing a bunch of dating—and damn, I was crazy about it. Even though I was preparing to enter grad school and had a ton of shit on my plate, my dating life took precedence over everything. I remember spending hours analyzing emails from guys with my girlfriends. What did it mean that he said we were on an "upswing"? Why would he only call post-midnight (duh)? What, for the love of god, should I wear!? I got my work done, but I would have ditched it if "he" called. It was a sorry state of affairs. I later realized that if I'd spent half the energy on my career and school stuff as I did on my relationships, I'd probably be the fucking president by now. Or at least on my second book.

Imagine if, for every panic attack over a date outfit or unreturned phone call, we instead stressed about our professional accomplishments or our personal development. Sounds silly, but it could make a huge difference. In a way, rejecting normative romantic expectations—even through simple acts like these—is revolutionary.

And while I'll probably continue to be a bit of a fool when it comes to my crushes, I won't make the mistake of prioritizing them at the expense of, dare I say, more important pursuits.

Again, don't get all pissy and assume I'm bashing those of you who are in love with love. I understand that feeling— believe me. But you have to admit, we're spending a hell of a lot of time focusing on other people when we could be mixing shit up.

Forever Boy Crazy

The romance industry is everywhere: Valentine's Day, dating (dating shows are enough on their own), magazines telling you how to land, keep, please your man. And no doubt, a lot of this stuff is massively fun. I'll admit it: I had a brief addiction to the reality show *Blind Date*. But that doesn't mean that it's not completely . . . vapid. Amazingly so, actually. Those shows play on the assumption that landing a man is all women care about. And I'd like to think that's a bunch of hooey.

If only pop culture agreed with me. I mean, dear lord, have you seen *The Bachelor?!* To me, that reality show epitomizes the false assumption that the only thing on gals' minds is marriage. To a rich hottie, preferably. If you haven't seen the show, or any of its various knockoffs, here's the quick summary: A group of young, beautiful women (like, twenty of them!) compete over one rich, hot guy. The ultimate goal is to get him to propose to you at the end of the show. Much airtime is given to showing the women fighting over the bachelor, fawning over all of the expensive dates and exotic locales, and eventually displaying their "true colors." You know, the kind that reveals that they're—gasp!—not just there for love.

Outside of all of the women's gross displays of desperation, "gold-digging," and downright nastiness to each other (which seem awfully contrived), the weirdest thing is that only the bachelor gets to do the rejecting—the assumption being that all the women involved would naturally want him; that not one of them would find him maybe a little annoying or maybe just not the guy for them. Again, forget chemistry and personality. He's rich and cute, so all women must want him. The underlying message is that while *he* cares about "true love," the women involved couldn't give a shit about what really matters—they just want to get married to anyone, so long as he's got cash and looks.

Sure, they had *The Bachelorette,* but let's be honest—it wasn't the same. And she wasn't rich—just hot. The men weren't portrayed as desperate goons catfighting for a woman's attention. Unlike the women on *The Bachelor,* they weren't positioned as morally vacuous and stupid.

Apparently, it's just women's job to be pathetic. And no matter who does the rejecting, guy or girl, it's always the gals on the show who are reinforcing awful stereotypes about women. (And don't tell me it's "reality." Please.)

Of course, this is just one example—one particular show that happens to be a pet peeve of mine. But the message is everywhere: Women want to get married (even if they have to trick someone into it); men want to avoid it and get laid as much as possible. It's *Cosmo* versus *Playboy*. Scary. And seriously, if I see one more quiz in a magazine that tells me how to tell if he likes me, I'm going to lose it.

Seriously, though, I used to be a bit of a magazine whore, so I understand no one is going to be giving up their *Glamour* anytime soon. (Though I must admit, *Glamour* and *Marie Claire* have gotten a lot better about covering "hard" issues recently.) Just a small suggestion: Try something a little different, like *BUST* or *Bitch* or *Ms.* They're good, I swear. And no fucking annoying quizzes.

Another peeve. If we're going to be subject to love and romance pretty much everywhere, could it at least be an accurate representation of coupledom? 'Cause somehow, in the fantasy world presented to us—beyond the white horses and princes and happily ever after—there are no gay people. Like, at all. Yeah, sure, there are cable shows depicting homolove, but the mainstream romantic image just isn't same-sex. And don't say *Will & Grace;* just don't. One show does not a movement make. We're making strides, that's for sure. But until women's mags start offering quizzes that tell you how to land your guy *or* gal, we're still in la-la land. I think we can all recognize that.

If you're still unconvinced that there's an overload of (heteronormative) love in the air, just think about Valentine's Day. 'Nuff said. Once those little cardboard hearts make their way into the drugstore windows, I start getting that sick feeling. You know, the feeling that whether you're dating someone or not, February fourteenth is going to be one

> 2006 Valentine's Day retail sales were expected to be $13.7 billion.

hell of an annoying day. Either you're a pariah for not having a significant (opposite-sexed) other, or you're subject to unrealistic romantic expectations. You know it's true. It's kind of like New Year's Eve—you expect so much out of the holiday that it always turns out to be a massive disappointment. That said, I still like flowers. That's why I've been known to buy myself an orchid on some V-Days. I frigging love orchids.

So, we may not be able to escape the romance industry—unless we're willing to forever give up television, magazines, movies, and everything else fun—but we can make decisions about how we live our dating life. And believe it or not, you can do it in a way that counteracts the annoying norm. It's not always easy, but it's worth it. And the truth is, doing *anything* that goes against the status quo is a step in the right direction. The most important thing? Do what feels right for you—not what everyone tells you is right.

Dating While Feminist

My friends and I love to discuss the ins and outs of feminist dating etiquette. It's not easy dating while feminist! Whether it's deciding who pays for dinner, who calls whom, or if your love interest is just too sexist to deal with, the road to feminist love is paved with obstacles. It's probably the case that it's as treacherous as nonfeminist love, but at least dating while feminist allows you to end up respecting yourself *and* the possibility of hanging out with a kick-ass significant other. Seriously, the coolest guys I've ever dated were the ones who were feminist-friendly, or even self-identified feminists.

My sister (who, shockingly, is also a feminist) and I used to joke that the easiest way to "test" a guy for dating appropriateness was to tell him you're a feminist right off the bat. If he makes a hairy-armpit joke, he's out. It's cool if he's curious, even better if he's impressed. The most common response we've gotten across the board? "But you don't *look* like a feminist!" Silly boys.

You can also try asking a date or someone you're interested in whom they voted for in the last presidential election. (Remember, no dating people who voted for anti-choice folks.) I also used to love to wear a shirt that read I DON'T

FUCK REPUBLICANS. That was a great weeder-outer, especially during election season. But in all seriousness, finding
someone who is beyond all the bullshit is no easy task. It's
even harder finding someone who doesn't fall for all of the
feminist stereotypes. Sometimes they'll think you're going to
be a man-hater (or that you are), that you're too opinionated, that you talk too much. These people are to be dumped
immediately. Waste no time on closet misogynists.

Then there are the folks who think the idea of dating a feminist is superneat—in the beginning. These faux
feminist-lovers will rave about how great it is to date a gal
with an opinion. They may even go to a feminist event with
you. Several months later, they'll tire of the novelty of dating
a cool girl and will wonder aloud where their dinner is.

But be patient.

Sooner or later, you'll find someone who gets it. And
when that happens, you'll thank me. I swear.

Okay, on to actual etiquette.

The whole "who pays?" argument is always tricky. It's
a subject that always generates craziness on Feministing. I
don't know why it's considered so controversial, honestly.
My position has always been: Whoever did the asking-out
pays. And when it comes to relationships, I've always gone
by the whoever-makes-more-money rule. Or just plain taking turns. Not so hard, right? When I was living with my
college boyfriend, there were times when he was broke and
I paid the rent. Later, he had tons of money and I had none,
so he would pay for everything. The idea that men should

pay for women just irks me. Believe me, I like free meals—I'm Italian, after all. But expecting a guy to pay for you all the time is the equivalent of saying that you need someone to take care of you. And hopefully that's not the case. You're not a child. You're not helpless. You can pay for your own meals. And even your date's if you're so inclined.

What also bugs me about the guy-always-paying model of dating is the expectation that you should get what you pay for. That somehow, you'll "owe" a guy (and we all know exactly what you owe him) for taking you out. This isn't to say that

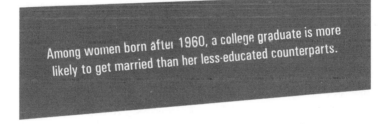

Among women born after 1960, a college graduate is more likely to get married than her less-educated counterparts.

some guys aren't just generous and nice and will expect nothing in return. And I'm also not saying that it's not occasionally nice to have someone—guy or gal—take you out on a date on their dime. But men's consistently paying for women sets up a power dynamic that women shouldn't be comfortable with.

This also relates to drink-buying when you're out. If a guy buys you a drink, all of sudden he thinks he's bought your time. I can't tell you how many times I've sat and listened to some jerk ramble on just because he bought me a $5 vodka tonic. Then, of course, I finally decided that someone's

FULL FRONTAL FEMINISM

buying me a drink didn't mean I had to hang out with him all night. I had more than one experience of getting shit for it from the buyer. "Hey, I bought you a drink; you can't go anywhere!" Ew. I'm all for chatting up someone who was nice enough to buy me a drink. But one drink doesn't mean I owe you my whole night. I think someone's offering to buy you a drink can be a nice gesture, and I don't think there's anything wrong with accepting (or telling them hells no, for that matter). But, let's be honest, it's kind of wack to *expect* drinks, just as it's in poor taste to expect someone to talk to you all night because you bought one.

A random note on Ladies' Night at bars: It's fun to get free or discounted drinks. Ladies' Night was my fave back in the day when I went out midweek. But, as I came to realize as I got a little older—and more sober—there is something inherently creepy about the idea of Ladies' Night. The bars want to bring in paying guys, and they figure the best way to do that is promise them a bar full of drunk-ass girls. It just seems predatory to me. End rant.

What I love about feminists (and this isn't me tooting our own horns, I swear) is our ability to take sexist crap and transform it into something awesome.

Take Valentine's Day. Inspired by Eve Ensler's award-winning play *The Vagina Monologues* and the resulting campaign to end violence against women, feminists on college campuses across the country started V-Day. On Valentine's Day, they perform the play, and proceeds generally go to a local organization that fights violence against women. Too cool.

And that's just one way young women are changing this nonsense around. It gets a little harder when you start talking about the biggest romance beast of them all—weddings. Some feminists are subverting the whole wedding thing as well—planning untraditional ceremonies, keeping their last names (thank god), and asking for donations to gay-rights organizations in lieu of gifts.

Killing Bridezilla

Wedding fever is the scariest disease I have ever seen. The big expensive ring. The big expensive dress. The big expensive party. It's excess at its best. And note that I didn't say "marriage fever." The obsession with getting married has somehow lost the whole rest-of-your-life vibe. For straight folks—especially women— marriage is supposed to be the ultimate destination. You spend your life dating toward it, worrying about it, and then arriving there and paying a hell of a lot of money for it. This isn't to say I'm against getting married. I think it's great if people want to make that kind of commitment to each other. What worries me is that young women are being taught that unless you have a Tiffany ring and a Vera Wang dress, your wedding and marriage are crap. And what happens to the women who get married and then find out that marriage is not all it's cracked up to be? As we've already figured out, women are still—still!—doing the majority of housework even if they have full-time jobs. And marriage is still being positioned as the "natural" thing people (women, especially) should want to do. We should want to get married and have the wedding; we should have been planning this since we were little girls and playing "bride" with pillow-cases over our heads like veils. And if it never really occurred to us to get married, well, clearly something is amiss.

Not to mention, should anyone really be all that excited about a privilege not everyone has? If marriage is such a super-fantastic institution, shouldn't all of us be able to partake?

The whole wedding insanity started bothering me when I first watched *A Wedding Story* on The Learning Channel a couple of years back. It's a cute show: It shows the bride and groom describing how they met, how the proposal went, and how crazy in love with each other they are. Aw. But the majority of the show is about the planning of the wedding and the wedding itself. It's not called *A Marriage Story,* after all. But shouldn't getting married be about, well, the marriage rather than the party? Not that wanting to have a nice wedding is a bad—or new—thing. But the cash aspect has changed significantly in recent years, and the focus on consumerism versus romance is kind of disturbing.

The show—the word, even—that epitomizes this all? *Bridezillas.* In case you're not the trashy pop culture whore I am, *Bridezillas* is a show that features brides basically losing their shit emotionally while planning their weddings. They go crazy spending money on ridiculous stuff and are major bitches along the way. (Okay, literally, I was watching *Bridezillas* while writing this, and, I shit you not, it featured a gay male couple. So now I slightly love the show.)

As much as I'd like to say that it's just the show that makes weddings look more monstrous than they actually are, the stats back up the *Bridezillas* ideal. A 2006 study showed that the average amount spent on U.S. weddings is almost $28,000. For a party. I'm sorry, but that's a down payment on a house. Not only is this a ton of money, but the amount couples spend on weddings has increased almost 100 percent

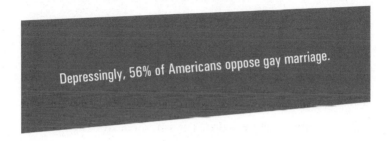

Depressingly, 56% of Americans oppose gay marriage.

since 1990. That includes the cost of engagement rings—which I have a *ton* to say about later—which has increased 25 percent over the same period.

Again, I'm all for a good party, but do we really have to spend this kind of money to prove to our friends and family how in love we are? And *why* do we feel compelled to spend so much? To keep up with our friends and the gross celebrity culture that shows folks spending hundreds of thousands on one night? Call me a hopeless romantic, but it seems to me that getting married should be about how much you love someone—not about how hot you look in a $5,000 dress. Just saying.

Of course, commodifying marriage is nothing new. Marriage hasn't always been about romance and love; it was about business arrangements, joining families together, and the like. And I'd be a terrible feminist if I didn't mention it was (is?) about passing ownership of women from dads to husbands.

It would be nice to think that this "ownership" aspect of marriage is dead and gone, but it still exists in various (and numerous) forms. You may not like me for saying this . . . but engagement rings piss me the hell off. It's a frigging dowry! Now, I like me some jewelry. And I like gifts. But the only purpose of an engagement ring is to show that you "belong" to someone, and that your man makes bank. You don't see men sporting engagement rings, do you? Recently, I was talking to my friend and fellow feminist blogger Amanda Marcotte about the engagement ring debacle. I mentioned that perhaps if men started wearing engagement rings too, we could put the whole controversy to bed. (Was this a desperate bid to reconcile my feminist sensibilities with my love of things sparkly? Um, more than likely.) Amanda pointed out that she thought engagement rings only got superpopular when wedding bands for men became the norm—the idea being that there always has to be something extra to mark women specifically as property. So if men started wearing engagement rings, next thing you know, ear tags for women (maybe with their fiancé's income stamped on them) would become popular. I'm joking, but you get the point.

On a personal level, I've been having an increasingly hard time with the idea of engagement rings. I'm at that age when my friends are getting engaged by the dozen—and a lot of my friends are guys. Frankly, I see the ridiculous amount of money they're spending, and the stress and the pressure they're under to prove their financial worth—and it just depresses me. I feel like shaking their significant others at times: "You're making us all look bad—we're not gold diggers!" But then I remember that the blame shouldn't be put on the women who buy in to this stuff. The wedding industry is tremendously powerful and wealthy, and the norms concerning engagement, marriage, and pretty much anything about heterosexual love relationships is pervasive like a mofo. It's impossible to escape. So it's kind of shitty to look down on women for simply partaking in romantic social norms. That said, it would be nice if we could start thinking about getting past this stuff and recognizing it as the materialistic distraction it is. I'm sorry, but so long as we keep buying in to the idea that we need to be bought, we're not going to think of ourselves as people deserving love and respect—just trinkets.

While at the end of the day I'm not going to fault someone for wanting a ring, there are certain things (and maybe because they don't have to do with jewelry) I can't get over. For the life of me, I will *never* understand why a woman today would change her last name. It makes no sense whatsoever. You want future kids to have the same last name as you and your hubby? Hyphenate! Or do something, anything, but change your last name. It's the ultimate buy-in of sexist bullshit. It epitomizes the idea that you are not your own person.

Eighty-one percent of women get married intending to change their last names, so clearly I'm of the minority opinion on this one. But seriously, where's the logic here? It's a pain in the ass to change your name (legally and all that), it represents an exchange of ownership (presumably dad's last name to hubby's), and you don't get to have your last name anymore! I don't know, maybe your last name is terrible and you can't wait to change it. Still, it irks me. Maybe because so many women still change their name without a second thought. As if we *have* to give in to the norms without a fight. So at the very least, please, if you get married, just think the last-name thing over. And besides, hyphenation is the new black.

To Have and to Hold (Unless You're a Homo)

Outside of all the other problems that go along with marriage as an institution—sexist past, the insane consumerist present—there's the small problem of not everyone being allowed to get married. I mean, if marriage is such an awesome and wonderful thing, shouldn't we all be able to do it?

The same-sex marriage debate has been quite the controversial topic since Republicans decided to make it an issue in 2004 when (sigh) Bush got reelected. You would think that with all the effort these folks put into getting straight people to marry, they would be overjoyed that a whole other section of the population wants to join in on the fun. But alas, homophobes abound in the government—and in the U.S. voting population, unfortunately.

After some cities started performing same-sex weddings (we love you, San Francisco, Portland, and New Paltz!), Massachusetts legalized same-sex marriage in 2004. That started a shitstorm of homophobia that went way beyond the presidential elections.

Lambda Legal Defense and Education Fund reports that thirty-eight states have since passed laws by state legislators banning same sex marriage; President Bush is even trying to push a constitutional amendment that would prevent same-sex couples from getting married (because apparently, the Constitution should be used to take away rights, not give them. Ugh.)

It's pretty unbelievable when you think about it: How can you legislate love? Hate to sound cheesy, but it's true.

And if you're thinking, *Well, there are always civil unions and partnerships* . . . I call bullshit. Civil unions don't carry the same legal benefits as marriage. According to NOW, same-sex couples are denied more than one thousand federal protections and rights, ranging from "the ability to file joint tax returns to the crucial responsibility of making decisions on a partner's behalf in a medical emergency."[1] These are rights that married couples do have. You know, cause they have The Sex that makes The Babies and are therefore acceptable. There are also financial issues that same-sex couples are prohibited from obtaining—like benefits and property inheritance. Not to mention the fact that gay parents have limited parenting rights if they're not the biological parent. You can't tell me that's not amazingly fucked up.

But for me, the biggest issue surrounding same-sex marriage is a pretty simple one—human rights. How can you relegate certain people (because of who they love!) to second-class citizenship because you think gays are icky? Give me a fucking break.

I think what this goes to show—outside of the unbeliev-able ignorance and hatred that some people have in their hearts—is that marriage isn't only about love.

For the same reasons the government is pushing mar-riage on women who are on welfare, they're trying to keep it away from same-sex couples. They see it as an ideologi-cal thing—a way to restore (enforce) their "traditional" val-ues. Whether we like it or not. Fun fact: In the same breath, President Bush managed to talk about his Healthy Marriage Initiative (the program that tells women on welfare that they don't need a job, they need a man) and define marriage as a heterosexual institution. In his 2003 statement on the cre-ation of Marriage Protection Week, he said:

☀ Marriage is a union between a man and a woman, and my administration is working to support the institu-tion of marriage by helping couples build successful marriages and be good parents. . . . To encourage marriage and promote the well-being of children, I have proposed a Healthy Marriage Initiative to help couples develop the skills and knowledge to form and sustain healthy marriages.[2]

Romantic, huh?

It just goes to show you how easy it is to take institutions like marriage and make them into something discriminatory and just plain wrong. Because so many of these ideas of mar-riage, romance, and love are built on sexism and consumer-ism, they're that much easier to pervert.

Reclaiming Romance

Clearly, romance has become the domain of the dollar—and the government. So I say let's take it back.

There's no reason we can't have fulfilling romantic lives without adhering to the bullshit standards that are set before us. Mix it up. Create your own standards and your own romantic norms.

Then that way, the next time you see some display of a played-out romantic ideal, you can laugh it off. Hopefully all while wearing your I DON'T FUCK REPUBLICANS shirt.

8

"REAL" WOMEN HAVE BABIES

Since writing *FFF,* I've had a daughter and gotten to experience firsthand how the world changes when you have children. I wrote in this chapter about the ways in which women's bodies—especially when they're pregnant or become mothers—are considered public property. It's a whole different ball game when you experience it yourself. For example, here's something I wrote while I was pregnant about people touching me: "Stop touching my stomach without my permission. It's presumptuous and it creeps me out. You wouldn't touch a non-pregnant person's belly without asking, so what makes you think it's okay to just lay hands on mine? I know you probably mean well and are excited about the baby and all, but please just ask first. (Especially because there's no socially acceptable way for me to tell you to stop without sounding like a killjoy.)"

Even when you have a child, the public property assumption doesn't stop. I've had people chastise me in public for bottle-feeding my daughter (as opposed to breastfeeding) and give me a sideways glance if I've mentioned that I'm traveling while she's at home with a sitter. The judgment that's heaped upon moms—often by other mothers, unfortunately—is unbelievable. This judgment, which can also take form politically and policy-wise, only becomes worse in marginalized communities. Who we consider a "good" mother is still inextricably linked to racism, classism, and heteronormativity. (And, of course, there's the assumption that all women want to become mothers in the first place!)

Whether it's repro rights, violence against women, or just plain old vanilla sexism, most issues affecting women have one thing in common—they exist to keep women "in their place." To make sure that we're acting "appropriately," whatever that means.

A huge part of keeping women in their place has to do with creating a really limited definition of what a "real" woman is like. And a ton of that what-makes-a-woman nonsense is attached to motherhood. Apparently, by virtue of having ovaries and a uterus, women are automatic mommies or mommies-to-be.

Now, don't get me wrong, I think motherhood is an awesome thing—if that's what you want. But there's something insanely disturbing about the idea that because I *can* have a baby, I *should* have a baby—and that this is something I should want to do more than anything in the whole wide world. And if I don't have that desire? Well, something is just plain wrong.

But of course the mommy pressure goes way beyond just popping them out. It's about what kind of mother you are, and anything less than perfect just won't do. If you work, you should be staying at home with your kids. If you're poor or on welfare, you should be working (sorry there's no affordable childcare, too bad). If you want to take time off from work to hang out with your kids, you're a liability, but if you don't, you're a bad mother. If you don't take perfect care of yourself while you're pregnant, you're a horrible person (and maybe even a criminal). If you don't want to get pregnant, you're unnatural. There's really no winning when it comes to motherhood.

Not only do women *have* to become mothers in order to be good women, we have to become "perfect" mothers. All while getting pretty much no appreciation for it.

Forced Motherhood

Let's face it—a lot of women want to be mothers, but there are also plenty of us who just don't want to have kids. But for some reason, that's seen as unnatural.

Women are supposed to want to have babies. It's our "natural" inclination. Several of my friends—who are in their late twenties—decided a while ago that kids just aren't for them. But whenever they express that sentiment to anyone in their lives, the reactions are insane. They're generally pooh-poohed with an, "Oh, you'll change your mind," or just incredulousness that anyone would decide *not* to have kids. (Never mind that men who don't have kids are just charming bachelors.) It forever bugs them that despite the fact that they've made an informed decision that's right for them, they're constantly being judged for it.

Of course, the idea that *all* women should be mothers is inexorably linked with issues of choice. Because our bodies

> A 2006 study published in *Birth: Issues in Perinatal Care* says that voluntary C-sections have a higher risk of death to newborn babies.

are not really our own—they're for making babies for the greater good. And if we don't, we're selfish.

The wackiest example I've seen of this idea lately is this movement of religious women who call themselves Quiverfull Mothers (like keeping your "quiver" full of babies—ick) and think that women should have as many kids as they can in order to build an army for god. And (naturally), they think that women should be submissive, and that "women's attempts to control their own bodies—the Lord's temple—are a seizure of divine power."[1] So essentially, your body isn't your own; it's god's. Now, of course this is an extreme example. But it isn't far off from what some policymakers think about women and motherhood.

When South Dakota tried to outlaw all abortion, for example, the task force in charge of discussing the ban came out with this gem:

⚬ It is simply unrealistic to expect that a pregnant mother is capable of being involved in the termination of the life of her own child without risk of suffering significant psychological trauma and distress. *To do so is beyond the normal, natural, and healthy capability of a woman whose natural instincts are to protect and nurture her child.*[2] [Emphasis mine.]

So you see, expectations about motherhood and what women *should* feel are used against us in all different areas of our lives—particularly when it comes to controlling our own bodies.

Treat Yourself Like You're Pregnant . . . Even If You're Not

A really disturbing aspect of this obsession with all things mommy is that most of it has nothing to do with the woman—it's all baby, all the time. We're just the carriers, after all. Sounds harsh, I know, but it's true. Even public policy reflects the idea that a woman's worth lies in her lady parts (the baby-making ones, not the fun bits).

In 2006, the Centers for Disease Control issued federal guidelines asking all women who are able to have babies (so, most women in their reproductive years) to treat themselves as pre-pregnant—even if they have no plans to have children anytime soon.[3] Seriously.

This basically means that any woman who is capable of getting pregnant should be taking folic acid supplements, not smoking, and keeping herself generally healthy—but not for herself, mind you, but for the baby (the one that doesn't exist yet).

The vessel will make sure to treat its uterus and surrounding matter with care for the preparation of the almighty fetus. The vessel puts the lotion in the basket.

You know, I'm all for being healthy—but I'd like to think of myself as a bit more than a potential baby-carrier. And I'm sure you would too. But unfortunately, this treatment of motherhood as having nothing to do with women is all too common. And it's getting scarier and scarier.

It's Never Too Early to Start Punishing Mothers

A new trend in sexism that's somewhere in between repro rights and perfect-mommy standards is going after pregnant women. For anything and everything.

A new wave of laws dedicated to "fetal protectionism" is popping up like crazy on a state level—but they're more about punishing pregnant women (and, by proxy, their babies) than about helping them.

Just a few examples: Arkansas legislators are considering making it a crime for a pregnant woman to smoke a cigarette;[4] a Utah woman was brought up on murder charges after refusing to get a cesarean section and giving birth to a stillborn boy;[5] a bill passed in the Idaho state senate would send pregnant moms to prison if they're caught using illegal drugs;[6] and laws in Wisconsin and South Dakota allow for arresting pregnant women for alcohol use.[7]

Now, don't get me wrong. I don't think anyone wants to see babies born addicted to drugs or harmed by alcohol or cigarettes. But all of these laws actually harm infants and their mothers, rather than help them. After all, healthcare in prison is atrocious, and if these bills become laws, the number of babies born in prison (which isn't exactly a drug-free zone) would increase significantly.

Lynn Paltrow, the executive director of National Advocates for Pregnant Women, wrote an article about this rash of new laws, noting that while we should be concerned with the health of pregnant women, we should not be lining up to punish them.

> ☀ Focusing on pregnant women as dangerous people who require special control or punishment inevitably undermines maternal and fetal health. Such measures divert attention from pregnant women's lack of access to health services, and deter them from seeking what little help is available.[8]

Wyndi Anderson, also of National Advocates for Pregnant Women, says that "if we really want to provide an opportunity for women to have healthy pregnancies, then we need to think about ways we can support women and their families."[9] You know, as opposed to making things even worse.

163

These laws are a slippery slope, part of a larger trend that trumps the rights of a fetus over those of women. And as Paltrow points out in her article, where do they stop?

Could the police arrest a woman who doesn't take pre-natal vitamins? Throw her in jail for playing sports? And now, with this "pre-pregnant" nonsense, how long will it be

Teenage pregnancy has gone done by 50% in the last 25 years. Yay birth control!

until women who aren't pregnant are charged with not tak-ing care of themselves (in preparation for The Fetus)? It's all just too much.

If this were really about helping pregnant women and their babies, laws would be, well, helping them—not punish-ing them. But of course, it's not about helping anyone. It's about vilifying women in the name of perfect motherhood.

Unauthorized Mothering

As much as society wants women to have babies, it's really only *certain* women who should be reproducing: straight, married, white women.

That's why you see organizations like CRACK out there advertising specifically in low-income black neighborhoods.

That's why states are trying to enact laws that would prevent unmarried women (lesbians, wink wink) from accessing reproductive technology to help them get pregnant without the almighty penis.

That Quiverfull movement? Part of their belief system is that they are helping to prevent "race suicide" by having nice white babies.

So it's important to remember that the expectation of motherhood is directed differently at different women. The myth of the black "welfare queen" having lots of babies for the "wrong" reasons is as alive as it ever was, as is the idea that gay people shouldn't have families (you know, 'cause they don't do it the "natural" way).

And when you see stories about the "mommy wars" (stay-at-home versus working moms), they're overwhelmingly about white upper-class women who can afford to argue about whether to stay home or not.

Just something to think about.

Mommy Doesn't Know Best

Once women make their own (hopefully) decision to have children, a whole new set of expectations and problems comes up.

Before they even have the kid—outside of the punishing-pregnant-women trend—women are subject to a whole medical profession telling them the best way to have their children.

An example? The rate of cesarean sections is at an all-time high in the United States: Almost 1.2 million C-sections were performed in 2005, up 27.5 percent from 2003.[10] And what does this have to do with women making decisions about their medical care? Well, it seems that a lot of women are being pushed into having the procedure because it's easier for doctors. Some hospitals have even banned vaginal deliveries after a woman has had a C-section in a previous pregnancy. (There's also a fear of malpractice suits if something goes wrong in a vaginal delivery.)

For example, Lani Lanchester decided that she didn't want a C-section with her second child; she had the procedure for her first birth and the recovery was difficult. Despite having a healthy pregnancy, Lanchester was told that her hospital had a policy change and was no longer allowing women who had had C-sections to deliver vaginally. Because of insurance complications, Lanchester couldn't go to another hospital. "It feels very violating to have unnecessary major surgery. . . . I had no options. But at the end, I got tired of fighting the insurance companies, the hospital, and the doctors."[11]

Given these policies and all the opposition to natural birth, it's no wonder that more and more women are questioning whether they want to give birth in hospitals at all, C-section or otherwise. As women tire of the impersonal hospital setting, in which they're made to feel unwanted, and even diseased, midwives and doulas are becoming increasingly popular. I'm all for giving birth in a comfortable environment surrounded by supportive people, not only because women should have as many options as they can when it comes to having a kid, but also because we shouldn't be made to fear the birthing process—as if we'll drop dead if we don't go to a hospital to have a baby.

Organizations like the New York–based BirthNet actually say that 90 percent of pregnancies are natural births that don't need hospital assistance.[12] They encourage the use of registered midwives, who can help women give birth at home or at a birthing center. (And by the way, a lot of midwife birthing centers are based in or around hospitals.)

But it's not over once you have the baby. Oh, no. Now enters a whole new set of problems, again relating to being the perfect mommy.

My pet peeve? Folks who rag on nursing mothers. This has been in the news a lot lately because moms are not taking shit anymore (and I love it). Moms—some of whom are calling themselves "lactivists"—are holding nurse-ins across the country to bring attention to stores and companies that won't let women breastfeed.

For example, a mom in Boston was asked to leave a Victoria's Secret dressing room because she was breastfeeding. Local mothers reacted by holding a nurse-in; the store ended up apologizing, and they got plenty of press.[13] Awesome. A woman was recently even thrown off a Delta flight when she refused to stop breastfeeding.[14] So we're supposed to be good moms and take care of our kids (and everyone knows the breast is best!), but when we want to do it in public—gross! You know, because boobies are for boys, not babies.

Some states, thankfully, have taken action by creating laws ensuring that breastfeeding women have rights.

35.7% of all births in 2004 were to unmarried women; 55% of the births among mothers ages 20–24 were to unmarried women. Some say it's because Americans are shunning marriage and just living together. Huh.

In fact, in a move to aid breastfeeding moms against those who find feeding babies objectionable, Kansas health officials decided to give out cards with a message: "A mother may breastfeed in any place she has a right to be."[15] If a woman is asked to leave a public place for breastfeeding, the back of the card has numbers where she can report the incident. Sweet.

The point is, this is the kind of shit that mothers have to put up with constantly—no matter how old their kids are. Whether it's breastfeeding, giving birth, work choices, childcare choices, or college choices, there's just no winning.

Pregnancy Is the New Black

I just had to mention the insanity that is celebrity pregnancy–watching these days. It's the new glamorization of motherhood. Whether it's the trend of "bump watching" in the tabloids (assuming that the post-lunch sandwich stomach is a bouncing baby-to-be) or the adoption craze, society loves it some celeb mommies.

Now there are even ads for nonalcoholic beer that feature "pregnant" models. I say "pregnant" 'cause the bellies are Photoshopped in. Gross.

I think our obsession with pregnancy and celebrities just goes to show how far the "perfect mommy" thing has gone. We look up to celebs for fashion, beauty, and style—and now we look up to them as parents. More than kind of weird, I know.

Underappreciated Mothers: The New Norm

For all the pressure women have on them to become perfect mommies, you would think that society would make it easy (or easier) on us. But hells no. Like I've mentioned before, there's a Mommy Wage Gap, problems with paying for child-care, and issues of negotiating work life with motherhood.

I mean, just the fact that women with children make seventy-three cents to a man's dollar (single mothers make fifty-six to sixty-six cents to a man's dollar), while women without children make about ninety cents to a man's dollar, is pretty nuts.[16] The wage gap is tied up with motherhood, and we're not even talking about it.

Not to mention, moms are just downright underappreciated. A recent study on motherhood by the University of Connecticut and the University of Minnesota shows that not only do moms feel undervalued by the people in their lives, but they also don't feel appreciated by society in general— nearly one in five moms said she felt less valued by society since becoming a mother.[17] Now that's screwed up.

A great organization (and website) that addresses these issues is MomsRising.org, run by Joan Blades and Kristin Rowe-Finkbeiner—authors of *The Motherhood Manifesto: What America's Moms Want—and What to Do About It.*

The organization, which has more than fifty thousand members and fifty national organizations aligned with it, aims to "build a more family-friendly America" through grassroots and online organizing. Its manifesto—which I think is fabulous—focuses on maternity and paternity leave; flexible work hours and options for parents; safe after-school

> The United States is one of two industrialized nations (the other being Australia) that doesn't provide paid leave for new mothers.

options for children; healthcare for all kids; quality, universal, affordable childcare; and fair wages for parents.[18] Seems simple and straightforward—and reasonable.

So why the hesitancy by society (and politicians) to make these seemingly simple things happen? The truth is, as much lip service as mothers are given, folks just don't care. If we cared about mothers and families, we would have universal childcare. If we cared about making motherhood easier, we would ensure that women and children got the healthcare they needed, got the flextime they needed, and got the support and—maybe most important—the trust they needed.

The sooner we start trusting women to make decisions about their lives and their families, the sooner we start valuing motherhood again.

Ask me about bra burning

9

I PROMISE I WON'T SAY "HERSTORY"

One of things I've been wondering a lot about concerning history and feminism is the way in which all of the incredible activism that's been happening online will be counted and archived. Will we only hear about the wins of major organizations? Or will there be some sort of record—some sort of feminist history somewhere—that includes Twitter campaigns, blogs, or Tumblr memes? It's not as simple as putting things in a real-life library anymore! So, as we move forward with all of our hard work, let's start to think about how we make sure it's remembered.

The history of feminism in the United States is generally thought of in an extremely limited way: Women got the vote, then some women burned their bras. Then it died 'cause women were equal. Done and done. Exciting stuff, huh?

Even the more complex version that's taught in women's organizations and classes often leaves out the racist and classist background of the movement. (Hey, we have to admit that shit.) Especially as everything stands right now in the feminist movement, there's a lot of back-patting and self-congratulation—as there should be, to some extent. But what we haven't been doing is being really honest about the less–PR friendly aspect of the feminist movement, or looking forward in a substantive way.

After all, if we can't be critical of ourselves and recognize our weaknesses, how can we be effective as a movement? The problem is, feminists are *so* used to people giving them shit—the constant backlash—that we've learned to focus on the positive. We're always on the defensive, for good reason. Feminists have become very good at anticipating backlashy comments and putting forward a united front, because we have to. But there's a way to do that while still remaining honest with ourselves.

American feminism—like a lot of social justice movements—has had plenty of growing pains. And we have to own them. Especially because many of those growing pains are still poking at us. Unfortunately, a lot of organized feminism these days is pretty damn cliquey—at least in terms of the "big" gals. National organizations, which are generally the public face of feminism, often don't represent the reality of the movement.

The same people who were running shit back then are running it now. (Time to pass the torch, ladies!) Not that

I blame them. You start something, you want to finish it. But one of the major problems with feminism today is its inability to recruit younger women and keep them interested. And this shouldn't come as a surprise to anyone: If you get younger women into feminism but then don't give them power or decision-making abilities, they're going to get real bored. Real fast.

So while I'm going to do my best to give you some background about how we got where we are today, I want to spend more time writing about where we're going. Because as important as feminism's history is, and as proud as we should be of our foremothers, the more important question is about how we move forward. Together.

We've Come a Long Way, Baby

It's difficult to say who the first feminists *really* were. I imagine women have been subverting sexism for as long as it's existed. But no one talks about the small things women do every day to buck the system, I suppose because it's impossible to measure. So when most people talk about feminist history, it's limited to the organized, popular movements.

If you're all-knowing about the "wave" history, feel free to skip this section. I don't want you to get bored. But if you're not, read on.

Most feminists discuss the movement's history in terms of waves: first, second, and third. Nowadays, the absence of a "fourth" wave seems to indicate a desire to end the wave terminology and just move forward without labels.

FIRST!

When folks talk about feminism's first wave, they're talking about women who fought for the vote. Think Elizabeth Cady Stanton and Susan B. Anthony. (If you didn't learn about them in school—at least—I might cry). Some mark the beginning of the first wave as the 1848 Seneca Falls Convention—when women got together in New York and created the Declaration of Sentiments and Resolutions, which outlined the issues and goals for a women's movement.

If you want to watch a good movie (with a somewhat unfortunate soundtrack) about the later part of the first wave, check out *Iron Jawed Angels*. It follows the fight for suffrage through the story of Alice Paul and Lucy Burns, who formed the National Woman's Party.

So, very long story made short: Women got the vote via the Nineteenth Amendment in 1920. Yeah, so it took them a long-ass time (wonder why . . .).

The problem with the way the first wave is generally talked about and taught is that it tends to ignore contributions by women of color and women who weren't all rich and privileged. It's all white, middle- to upper-class women

Feminists never really burned their bras. That rumor started after women protesting the 1968 Miss America Pageant threw their bras in a trashcan.

all the time. (You'll see that this is a trend through the waves.) In fact, the most famous suffragettes turned out to be a tad racist. Stanton and Anthony got all pissed that black men got the vote over white women and forged some pretty unsavory alliances with groups that opposed enfranchisement for black people and even said that the vote of white women (of "wealth, education, and refinement") was needed in order to combat the "pauperism, ignorance, and degradation" of voting immigrants and men of color.[1] Lovely.

Fact is, women of color were fighting their own battles at the time and not getting nearly enough recognition. One speech that (thankfully) gets a lot of play is Sojourner Truth's "Ain't I a Woman?" delivered in 1851 at the Women's Convention in Ohio.

❋ That man over there says that women need to be helped into carriages, and lifted over ditches, and to have the best place everywhere. Nobody ever helps me into carriages, or over mud puddles, or gives me any best place! And ain't I a woman? Look at me! Look at my arm! I have ploughed and planted, and gathered into barns, and no man could head me! And ain't I a woman? I could work as much and eat as much as a man—when I could get it—and bear the lash as well! And ain't I a woman? I have borne thirteen children, and seen most all sold off to slavery, and when I cried out with my mother's grief, none but Jesus heard me! And ain't I a woman?[2]

Awesome.

Now, of course, it's great that women got the vote and that so many women fought for it—hard. But we have to take an honest look at history. Because unfortunately, this dismissive nonsense about anyone other than educated white women would repeat itself, to some extent, later on in feminism.

SECOND!

The second wave is probably the most well-known time period in feminist history. Or at least the most talked about. (Bra burning! Hairy legs! Lesbians!) It's also the most misrepresented, in my opinion.

When people think about 1970s feminism, they think Gloria Steinem and burning bras. Steinem was real, braburning was not. The mainstream, popularized women's movement back in the day started out of a desire to get out of the home. Women felt trapped by the '50s-housewife model set before them, which laid out a life that pretty much entailed getting excited only about ovens and kids and bringing your man a drink when he got home from work. Woohoo!

Betty Friedan's *The Feminine Mystique* took on "the problem that had no name" (women being sick and tired of being maids).[3] Friedan was also a founding member of NOW, which was created in 1966. The organization's original statement of purpose, written by Friedan, declared that "the time has come for a new movement toward true equality for all women in America, and toward a fully equal partnership of the sexes."[4] The statement also focused on the issues that second-wave feminism is most known for: women working outside the home, the wage gap, sex discrimination, women's representation in the government, and fighting traditional notions of motherhood and marriage. Obviously, we're still fighting some of those battles (okay, all of them), but orgs like NOW did a hell of a lot for women on these issues.

But (there's always a but) what *isn't* part of NOW's celebrated accomplishments is the other side of the organization's past—and, by proxy, that of the mainstream second wave. After its inception, NOW was accused of being homophobic and in later years was criticized as speaking only to issues that affected middle-class white women.

Afraid to be stereotyped as "man-haters," NOW distanced themselves from lesbian issues in the late 1960s. Friedan even called lesbians a "lavender menace" to the larger women's movement. *The lesbians are coming! The lesbians are coming!* It's essentially the same nonsense that the suffragettes pulled—afraid that the radical notion of black people getting votes or lesbians defining feminism would kill the mainstream friendliness of the movement. Pshaw.

Criticism of NOW as being a middle-class white women's organization—along with the second-wave movement as a whole—isn't exactly a new trend. After all, much of the movement was based on the idea that women should be working outside the home. But low-income women and women of color had already been working outside (and inside) the home—they had to!

Some cool stuff that came out of the second wave: *Ms.* magazine was founded by Gloria Steinem and run by Robin Morgan and Marcia Ann Gillespie (among others);[5] *Roe v. Wade* was decided, and women obtained the right to get abortions;[6] Title VII of the Civil Rights Act was passed, making employment discrimination illegal on the basis of sex, as was Title IX, which banned discrimination in education;[7] Angela Davis (yes, just her—she rocks);[8] Susan Brownmiller wrote *Against Our Will* about the culture of rape; feminists fought for increased awareness of violence against women;[9] Alice Walker coined the term "womanist" ("a black feminist or feminist of color. . . . Usually referring to outrageous, audacious, courageous or willful behavior.");[10] lesbian theory

> Suffragette Edith Garrud taught martial arts to other women as a way to protect themselves against violent police officers.

gained popularity;[11] and the "sex wars" happened, in which anti-porn and not-so-anti-porn feminists clashed.[12] Shit, I could go on forever—so make sure to check out the resources at the end for more stuff. Now, I may catch some flak for not expounding more on the successes of the second wave and telling you *everything*. But the thing is, there are about a million books out there for that. Go read them. And I'm not being trite—I think we owe a lot to our foremothers. So much in fact, that not getting down to business would be a disservice.

THIRD!

The third wave (which I suppose I'm a part of) also has a bunch of unsavory stereotypes attached to it. We're supposedly the flighty, unserious feminists. 'Cause we like makeup and heels and talk about pop culture. Silliness. But to a certain extent, that's what makes the third wave kind of fabulous. We're still working on the serious issues, but we understand that the things that don't necessarily seem integral (pop culture, for example), well, are.

When I think third wave, I think of academic stuff, like different feminist theories (queer, postcolonial). But the less dry stuff associated with third-wavers is magazines like the fabulous *BUST* and *Bitch*, books like *Manifesta*, and (swoon) Kathleen Hanna scrawling SLUT across her stomach.

Of course, reclaiming words like "slut," "bitch," and "cunt" doesn't necessarily sit well with everyone. There's the misconception that, somehow, using words that have traditionally been used to disparage women means we're falling in line with sexism. But what young women are really doing is taking the power out of those words by making them our own.

The same argument can be made for things like makeup and high heels. There are young feminists who get dolled up and say that this can be empowering. That's cool with me, though some (usually older) feminists say we're fooling ourselves. The thing is, I'm a fan of makeup and heels—and while I don't think that makes me any less of a feminist, I don't think it makes me any more of one, either.

I *know* that certain things I enjoy—traditional "feminine" things like makeup—are created by a system that says I'm not good enough without it. Blogger Jill Filipovic (of Feministe) nails it:

> ☀ I like my mascara, and I'm not going to waste time feeling bad about it, but I'm also not going to convince myself that long eyelashes are totally empowering and other women would be so much happier and more empowered if only they could have a makeover. I'm also not going to be spoken down to by women who should be my allies as they try and tell me that my behavior is unequivocally "wrong" and anti-feminist.[13]

The problem is, there's still a lot of infighting—particularly of a generational kind—about what a "real" feminist is. Honestly, I'm so fucking sick and tired of people telling me how to be an appropriate feminist—or what a feminist looks like. In the same way it's stupid to say that all feminists are hairy man-haters, it's stupid to say that women who rock heels and mascara aren't hardcore enough or are acquiescing to sexism.

Yes, we should analyze why we do the things we do and how they're related to sexism, but bashing each other in feminist pissing contests is pretty much the dumbest thing ever. Having a feminist judge you for what you look like or choose to do aesthetically is no different from having a sexist man do it. Except maybe for the damage it does to the movement.

The same thing goes for opinions on controversial issues like porn. Some are going to say that if you're not against porn, you're not feminist enough (this tends to happen a lot in second-wave/third-wave arguments). Everyone has their own version of feminism, everyone has their idea of what feminism is. It's not so important that we all agree all the time as it is that we all respect each other's opinions. How else can we move forward without killing each other?

This isn't to say that the third wave is all pop culture all the time, or all generational tension. To a large extent, the third wave is a response to the backlash (must read: Susan Faludi's *Backlash*[14]) that came about after the second wave. Third-wave feminists are as "serious" as those who came before us, really. What I love about the third wave is that we've learned how to find feminism in everything—and make it our own.

A note on academic feminism: So, I have a master's degree in women's and gender studies. And my time in grad school and in academia was invaluable in a lot of ways. It helped me develop my feminist identity and gave me a firmer understanding of my politics. That said, academic feminism isn't for me. I like activism. My parents didn't go to college, but my mom is the person who really got me into feminism. (Though grudgingly at first.) I remember really wanting to go to a pro-choice march in D.C. when I was in junior high, but the idea of having to hang out with my mom for the week-

end was too dorky to stand. I went anyway, and despite my
crankiness at having to do all the tourist stuff and my teenage nastiness whenever my mom wanted to take a picture of
us in front of some monument, I had a fantastic—and life-
changing—time. Seeing so many women mixing it up and not
taking shit from the horrible anti-choicers on the sidelines of
the march was all I needed to see to know that feminism was
for me. When I started coming home from grad school with
ideas and theories that I couldn't talk to her about, academic
feminism ceased to be truly useful for me. I think feminism
should be accessible to everybody, no matter what your education level. And while high theory is pretty fucking cool, it's
not something everyone is going to relate to.

What Now (NOW)?

The state of feminism right now is debatable. Some folks are
still saying it's dead, while we feminists keep on trucking.
Like I've said before (and I'll say again), young women are
rocking shit when it comes to the feminist movement. It kills
me when people say young American women aren't interested in feminism or politics, because most of the feminists
I know are women under thirty, and they're pretty seriously
into reproductive rights, poverty alleviation, the war, and
plenty of other social justice issues. But when it comes to the
media, the public face of feminism isn't a young one. Neither
is the face at the head of the table.

I've worked for a bunch of feminist organizations, some
national, one international. And in the last couple of years,

I've gotten more and more involved in popular U.S. feminism. And as much as I love it (to death), it still has its fair share of problems. The one that comes up the most for me—because of the work I do on Feministing—is the young-woman problem.

Young women are involved in every aspect of the feminist world I live in—running blogs, printing zines and magazines, and even founding small grassroots organizations. Young women are at the helm of a ton of feminist projects. But when it comes to more well-known organizations (and places that get the big money), younger women are pretty scarce, at least in decision-making positions.

I love anecdotes, so here's a good one on this very subject: The year 2006 marked NOW's fortieth anniversary; it was also the first time I ever attended one of its conferences. Shameful for a lifelong feminist, I know. NOW is a powerhouse organization. It's the go-to place for feminist quotes in the media, it has chapters all over the place, and it claims five hundred thousand dues-paying members. That's huge.

So I attended as a speaker and sat on a panel about feminism and blogging. Still—I'll admit it—I was a bit skeptical going in. I had heard rumors about previous conferences and

Mary Shelley, who wrote Frankenstein, was the daughter of one of the first feminists—Mary Wollstonecraft.

was halfway expecting to walk into some sort of retro hand-mirror/vagina workshop. (Don't worry, I didn't.)

A twenty-four-year-old feminist I know—who doesn't want me to use her name because she works with an organization affiliated with NOW—had painted a less-than-flattering picture of the 2005 conference. My friend was all set to be on a panel, but when she checked in, NOW officials told her that her "title" wasn't prestigious enough for her to speak. Harping on her title was just another way to say she was too young. "There was concern from NOW that I wasn't a serious enough speaker, partly because of my age and partly because my job title wasn't on par with the credentialed speakers I was scheduled to sit with." She was only allowed to remain on the panel after her superior called to complain. Ouch, right?

Thankfully, when I attended the conference, NOW was holding a Young Feminist Summit to ensure that younger women had a space to discuss their issues. My only complaint about the experience was the bad graffiti font on the conference webpage and some of the hackneyed "young" language: "We will be headin' to Albany, New York, and hangin' at the Crowne Plaza Albany Hotel. . . ." Apparently young feminists aren't fond of the letter g. But, hey, you can't fault them for trying.

And you know, this wasn't the only conference that has had this kind of problem. I went to a Feminist Majority Foundation conference once (it's the organization that owns *Ms.* magazine) that brought hundreds of college feminist activists to D.C. Awesome, right? It could have been, but the whole conference was the young activists being talked at! No time for socializing, no workshops, hardly even time for questions.

I'm not trying to hate, I'm really not. I know we all do our best. But I honestly think that if our foremothers want feminism to stay alive and kicking, they have to be willing to hand over the reins. At least to some extent. We also have to throw ourselves out there. When you see an article about feminism being dead, write a letter to the editor! Join a local women's organization—or start your own. 'Cause unless we prove otherwise, they're just going to keep saying that young feminists don't exist.

Moving Forward

I don't know what feminist organizing will look like in the years ahead. I'd like to think it will look like a lot of things.

I think organizations like NOW and Feminist Majority Foundation may no longer be at the forefront of feminism. Many national organizations focus more on D.C. lobbying than activism, in my humble opinion. Yes, I know they're activist organizations, but I see more activism from local groups than I do from national organizing lately. Not that that role is unimportant—it is. But the younger women I speak to see feminism going in a different direction—actually, a lot of different directions.

Thirty-one-year-old Joanne Smith, founder of the Brooklyn-based organization Girls for Gender Equity, says that the future of feminism "starts at home on a grassroots, community level. There has to be an intersection of 'The Hill and The Hood'; the current disconnect of [feminism on the Hill] creates a false sense of achievement or advancement in a movement that must be sustained and felt by everyone, or at least a majority of the oppressed."[15] I think this is brilliant, and right on point. Feminism has to be about accessibility—both in how we present it and how we do it.

Amanda Marcotte, blogger for Pandagon.net (and friend of mine), says that blogging is a great new way to look at feminist activism, especially because it's the realization of the old feminist adage "the personal is political." Amanda says that the awesome thing about blogs is that they "tear down so many of the obstacles that made it hard for individual women's stories to get an audience. The personal touch makes blogging a fertile ground for doing the hard work of waking people up to sexism and getting them committed to fighting it."

Not shockingly, I agree. I think feminist blogs are just about the best way ever to get news about women with smart (and smartass) commentary. A lot of the work I've done with Feministing has informed my activism and made me think in new ways about how to be a feminist and organize around women's issues. And for me, the most important component of my work and what I get involved in lies in its accessibility.

The great thing about doing online activism, especially blogging, is that it builds a community that you can't get anywhere else. If you're in some small town with no NOW chapter, or you're in a high school where no one else calls themself a feminist, you can go to a website and get involved and talk with people from all around. I love that.

I also think that local organizing has done more for feminism than people give it credit for. Yes, big protests in D.C. are great. But changing a local law, or even a school mandate, is incredibly important. Plus, it's easier to see the effects of activism when it's in your face and on your home turf.

At the end of the day, no matter what the form, any feminist activism is all good by me.

And despite the problems in feminism's history, I think we're a great big fucking force to be reckoned with. Especially when we're up front about our limitations. The real power of feminism isn't in our numbers or our public image; it's in the quality and diversity of the women involved. We don't need the rhetoric of sisterhood to make a difference—we already are.

10

Real men are feminists

BOYS DO CRY

One of the questions I get asked most often when I'm speaking on college campuses is what feminists can do to get more men involved. I find it such an interesting question because it both acknowledges that men's participation is important to feminism, but it also reveals a little bit of ignorance—because men are already involved in feminism, we just don't see them as much. Thanks to blogs and online forums, there are more male feminists making their voices heard than ever before. Men understand that these issues impact them as well—that patriarchy and double standards hurt them—and they want things to change. But in a more general sense, there also has to be a move to evangelize feminism to men who don't already consider themselves feminists. That's a tougher sell—because as much as men are hurt by sexism, they also benefit from it. I continue to believe that the best thing we can do is to prop up more male feminist voices—voices like Byron

Hurt and Jackson Katz. Men who can speak to other men. It remains true that feminism is largely a movement of women, but it shouldn't be and it doesn't have to be.

Be a man. Boys don't cry. Boys will be boys.

Men are affected by sexism too, but it's not often talked about—especially among men themselves. That's where feminism should step in.

The same social mores that tell young women that they should be good little girls are telling guys to be tough, to quash their feelings, and even to be violent. Their problems are our problems, ladies. Men aren't born to rape and commit violence. Men aren't naturally "tougher" emotionally. These gendered expectations hurt men like they hurt us.

I mean, really, can you imagine what it must be like to know that one of the only ways to demonstrate your "masculinity" is to do violence to someone else? To never let your guard down? Seems pretty goddamn awful to me.

Feminism can help men too, but only if they're open to it. We can't have a fully successful feminism if we're missing half the population. The thing is, how can we relay the super-fabulous stuff feminism is made of to the men in our lives?

I am by no means an expert on masculinity. There are great people doing amazing work on how sexism hurts men—like academic and masculinity expert Michael Kimmel and organizations like Men Can Stop Rape. I'd highly recommend checking these folks out if you're looking for in-depth information on masculinity.

in the role of the castrating mother. The result resembles a childlike fantasy of manhood that is endowed with the perks of adulthood—money, sex, freedom—but none of its responsibilities.[1]

Some say that this goes beyond pop culture silliness where *Maxim* magazine is king. In 2005, Rebecca Traister wrote about "listless lads," men who "are commitment-phobic not just about love, but about life. They drink and take drugs, but even their hedonism lacks focus or joy. . . . They exhibit no energy for anyone, any activity, profession, or ideology."[2] Traister theorizes that maybe this is a crisis in masculinity—where men don't want to be men.

But what does that mean, anyway?

Snips and Snails?

It seems unclear what "being a man" actually is. Is it simply *not* being a woman? Or is it something more?

According to Michael Kimmel, there are "rules of manhood":

- ☼ No sissy stuff, that's the first rule. You can never do anything that even remotely hints of femininity. The second rule is to be a big wheel. You know, we measure masculinity by the size of your paycheck, wealth, power, status, things like that. The third rule is to be a sturdy oak. You show that you're a man by never showing your emotions. And the fourth rule is give 'em hell. Always go forward, exude an aura of daring and aggression in everything that you do. And this model of masculinity has been around for an awfully long time.[3]

My thoughts on men and feminism are really just starting to be formed, but it's too important a topic to not get into it. Especially now, in a world where what it means to be "a man" has the potential to damage both men and women. Whether it's a consequence of the way that masculinity is used during wartime, or the way it's presented in pop culture—something just isn't right.

Without dissecting how masculinity standards affect men, we'll never be able to comprehensively address sexism and how it affects women. They're linked like a motherfucker. Besides, imagine how much easier it will be to develop male allies in feminism when they realize that they have something to gain from the movement as well.

Men Should Act Like Men

A commercial for Milwaukee's Best beer shows three guys digging a ditch in a back yard (can you smell the testosterone?). When a bee buzzes too close to one of the men, he frantically tries to wave it away while giving off a little high-pitched (you know, girlie) scream. His friends look on in horror. A huge can of Milwaukee's Best falls from the sky and

> Read this book: *Manhood in America: A Cultural History,* by Michael S. Kimmel.

crushes the offending man—who clearly is too femmey to live. The voice-over says, "Men should act like men." The same thing happens to another man who dares to soak up his pizza grease with a napkin. The moral of the story? Act like "a girl" and be killed by giant beer cans. Lovely.

What I find truly interesting about this commercial—and this limited view of what it means to be a man in general—is that masculinity is defined as whatever *isn't* womanly. So long as you're not acting like a girl (or a gay!), you're all good.

It's kind of along the same lines as that "what's the worst thing you can call a girl/guy?" exercise. The idea being that there is nothing worse than being a girl, and that being a man is simply the polar opposite of whatever "woman" is. So really, masculinity as it's defined in our society is ridiculously tied up in sexism. How sad is that?

So back to "men should act like men." I think the Milwaukee's Best commercial is so telling—it really does represent the current state of masculinity in a lot of ways. Not only does it define what it means to be a man by pitting it directly against girlishness, but it also implies that what's really important is that you "act" like a man. In a way, the commercial recognizes masculinity as a performance. So even if you are freaked out by bugs or don't want nasty grease on your pizza—suck it up and act like men "are supposed" to. Creepy, right?

But of course, expecting guys to "act" like men isn't limited to beer commercials—it's everywhere. How many times have you heard "Boys don't cry," or "Be a man"? Or even

my personal favorite, especially when it was said to me as a kid, "Don't be a girl."

The new trend, however, seems to be deviating from manhood altogether, and instead fetishizing boyhood.

Men Should Act Like Boys

Something kind of new in American masculinity—at least in terms of pop culture—is the resurgence of boyhood as the cool standard. Like, back in the day, being a man meant taking care of your family and having a good job and all that. Now, at least if you look at commercials and television shows and the like, it seems that the ultimate way to be a man is to stay a boy.

You know what I mean—the new cool is this "bros over hos" mentality that seems to be inundating our culture. Just think of all the commercials in which perpetual boyhood is the ultimate—where playing cards, watching football, drinking beer, and picking up chicks is the norm (even for "older" guys), and girlfriends and wives are annoying, nagging, distractions from fun.

In a March 2006 article entitled "Men Growing Up to Be Boys," Lakshmi Chaudhry says that an "infantilized" version of manhood is making its way to the mainstream:

❉ These grown men act like boys—and are richly rewarded for it. . . . Where traditional masculinity embraced marriage, children, and work as rites of passage into manhood, the twenty-first-century version shuns them as emasculating, with the wife cast

Kimmel describes it as "relentless pressure on men." I would imagine so. I can't imagine it's easy living that way. But unfortunately, this limited view of what it means to be a man truly fucks up the way men treat women.

Kimmel says that feminist-hating can be tied to masculinity as well. Because for men who are holding on for dear life to the traditional idea of what it means to be a man, feminism is a real threat—because it asks people to question traditional gender roles. He also believes that "manliness" can be tied to violence against women: "Men tend to be violent against women when they feel that their power is eroding, when it's slipping."[4] Ugh.

But this seems par for the course in terms of feminist backlash. Feminism changed things around in a lot of ways, and that is scary as hell to a lot of men—because they benefit from sexism. Sexism means that they're the ones with the power, with the rights, and with their dinner made every night. It's no wonder feminism scares the shit out of them.

Feminist Phobia

My first real taste of feminist phobia came when I taught Intro to Feminisms at SUNY Albany in upstate New York. I taught the class as part of a teaching collective program in which undergraduates could teach other undergraduates. So I was pretty psyched, but not so much with all of my students.

One guy, who was my age, took the class just to be disruptive. I knew it wasn't going to go well when, on the first day of class, we asked everyone to write their names on a piece of paper and hang it from their desks so we could all talk roundtable-style, and the guy wrote WOMAN HATER.

The semester was pretty miserable, with him trying to make me feel like shit at every turn. He wrote "Jessica is a bitch" on every test he handed in. He showed up at the anti-rape rally Take Back the Night to tell me that he had had sex with a girl when she said no (but that she liked it). He even had occasion to wander past my apartment drunk one night, just to yell out not-so-nice things. At the time, I just thought he hated me because he was a fucked-up person. Looking back, I realize that this guy was terrified of what he was being confronted with in class. It was going against everything he had ever learned, and his immediate reaction was to lash out. Plus, he was just a dick. He was acting out and felt he could without consequence because I was a woman his age—not an authority figure.

Since I've started Feministing, I've seen similar reactions online. We've gotten our fair share of hateful comments on the site, but none have compared to the vitriol spewed our way from a group of guys on the Internet who call themselves "men's rights activists."

Basically, their deal is that they blame feminism for everything from not being able to get dates to increasing crime rates. Weird stuff. Some of them hated what we were doing so much that they created a parody site modeled after Feministing! They stole our logo (though they made it look like she was fingering herself—classy), our name, and put this tagline on it: "Because women are never sexist. So there." Uh huh.

A great organization, Men Can Stop Rape, created this awesome website: Masculinities in Media: http://mencanstoprape.org.

They posted articles every day and even talked to each other in comments using female pseudonyms and language they thought feminists would use: "You go grrrl!" Yeah, I know. It was amazing to me that anyone would spend so much time creating and keeping up a site that no one really looked at or read besides their small group of online buddies. Besides, why weren't they out being active on behalf of men?

Again, it's the fear of feminism. They are terrified by the idea that women could actually be autonomous people with opinions. Interestingly, they blame feminism for ruining American women; on one of their websites (which has the lovely header "Ameriskanks suck"), they often discuss how Asian women are "real women" because they adhere to traditional gender roles. I won't even get into how dumb and racist that is, but the idea is that the perfect woman is one who doesn't, you know, talk back or have opinions.

This kind of misogyny (and yes, I do think a hatred of feminists is based in an overwhelming hatred of women) is unfortunately fairly widespread. There is just something about feminism that really pisses some guys off. Us gals from Feministing have actually received death threats, threats to cuts off our breasts (seriously), and threats of rape. Which is insane. But it's because feminism is powerful. If these same men who hate feminism so much weren't threatened by it and its power, they wouldn't waste their time creating sites, causing disturbances, and emailing threatening letters.

In a way, this fear of feminism is a testament to its strength.

When I had that kid in my Intro to Feminisms class, I used to think that if only he would really try to understand feminism, it could really help him. Because it was clear that he was looking for something. And at times I felt that way about our online "admirers." The truth is, some guys will never be open to feminism because misogyny is just too ingrained in them. Which is sad. But that doesn't mean that there aren't amazing men out there who support the cause.

Boys Will Be Feminists

Can men be feminists? Hell yeah; I've been lucky in my life to be surrounded by feminist men (hi, Dad!) and I see the difference it makes, so I'm all for men joining in on the fun, and I believe we need male allies. But not everyone agrees. Some feminists think that the movement needs to be woman-centered, and I can understand this hesitancy to include men. There is a fear that they wouldn't be willing to learn, and

Check out the organization Dads and Daughters, whose tagline reads "making the world safe and fair for our daughters": www.dadsanddaughters.org. Awww.

that they would try to take shit over, because they're used to leading. I even have friends who take issue with men calling themselves feminists. They think that women need a word all their own, and that only someone who experiences life as a woman can truly understand feminism.

So, some guys call themselves "pro-feminist" as a way to stand in solidarity with feminists without co-opting the word/movement. As far as I'm concerned, they can call themselves whatever they want, so long as they're down to do the feminist work.

Self-identified pro-feminist blogger and academic Hugo Schwyzer says it's imperative that men mentor other men in order to spread a nonsexist message.

> ☀ We owe it to them to make it clear that we have grown up with the same pernicious cultural influences that have taught us to objectify women. They need to know what tools we ourselves have used to change our behavior, and they need to know—in detail—how we live out egalitarian principles in our relationships with women. We can't preach gender justice; we have to live it out in our actions and we have to be willing to do so publicly, as role models.[5]

Unfortunately, it's not just men like Hugo who are trying to reach out to younger men.

Traditional Gender Roles on Crack

The same conservative messes that are telling young women that they have to be chaste, married, and popping out babies are telling young men that they have to be strong, be "soldiers."

James Dobson, daddy of the terrifying conservative religious group Focus on the Family, wrote a book called *Bringing up Boys* in which he tells parents how to raise their male children. A lot of it is concerned with nurturing boys' "natural" masculinity and making sure they don't turn out to be homos. Seriously. The Focus on the Family website (which promotes Dobson's book at every turn) says much the same thing:

> ❂ God designed boys to be more aggressive, excitable, and wild in their behavior. Despite the claims made a generation ago, boys are different. . . . To help a boy develop a healthy gender identity, make sure he receives appropriate affection, attention, and approval from his father (or, in the father's absence, a trustworthy male role model).[6]

There's even a section on "Countering Radical Feminism's Agenda"![7] The idea is that boys need their "masculine" side praised and their "feminine" side quashed.

Is the Military the Ultimate in Masculinity?

I couldn't write about men and masculinity without at the very least mentioning militarization and war. They're all too tied up with each other not to talk about it. Something superfucked up that will give you a good idea of why I'd feel remiss if I didn't write about militarization: During the Gulf

War (and who knows how many other wars), Air Force pilots watched porn movies before they went off on bombing missions in an attempt to "psyche [sic] themselves up."[8] Ugh. But that's par for the course for an institution that relies on the feminization of the enemy as a way to dehumanize them.

Feminists who study men and the military are quick to point out that the military itself is built on sexist ideals. Cynthia Enloe, a professor and an expert on feminism, militarization, and globalization, writes frequently about how militarization is dependent on women in "supporting" roles—whether as military wives or prostitutes on military bases.[9] Interesting stuff (though disturbing).

Even Amnesty International reports that women are disproportionately affected by war:

> ❋ [T]here is still a widespread perception that women play only a secondary or peripheral role in situations of conflict. . . . The use of rape as a weapon of war is perhaps the most notorious and brutal way in which conflict impacts on women. As rape and sexual violence are so pervasive within situations of conflict, the "rape victim" has become an emblematic image of women's experience of war.
>
> [W]omen and girls are targeted for violence, or otherwise affected by war, in disproportionate or different ways from men.[10]

Clearly, this is a huge issue, one that requires a lot more conversation than I can fit in this book. So this is just something to get you thinking.

Men Moving Forward

I think it's clear that everything—from social norms to pop culture—presents an insanely limited definition of masculinity, one that not only does damage to men, but harms women as well. So what to do now?

Robert Jensen, a journalism professor at the University of Texas, argues that the whole concept of masculinity as we know it has to go, because it creates a life for men that is marked by "endless competition and threat" and a quest for control and domination:

> ✸ No one man created this system, and perhaps none of us, if given a choice, would choose it. But we live our lives in that system, and it deforms men, narrowing our emotional range and depth. It keeps us from the rich connections with others—not just with women and children, but other men—that make life meaningful but require vulnerability.[11]

Men's lives are being damaged by sexism—we can't separate it out from how sexism affects women. Because every time someone calls a guy a "pussy" or a "mangina," every time someone tells a little boy not to "throw like a girl," the not-so-subtle message is that there is something inherently wrong with being a woman. And that's a message I think we could all live without.

The text on the t-shirt reads: "Shove your bullshit beauty standards"

11

BEAUTY CULT

One of the most powerful blogs I've seen crop up regarding beauty is the "Stop Hating Your Body" Tumblr. It encourages women to "join the body peace revolution" by posting pictures (if they want to) of their bodies and to describe the various struggles they've had—but also to talk about why they think their bodies are beautiful. In a culture that so often asks women to post naked or half-clothed pictures of themselves for scrutiny or sexual objectification, this blog is a great subversion of that.

Similarly, the Tumblr site "Disabled People Are Sexy" turns what "traditional" beauty means on its head. We need to shift our beauty standards so they are not so narrow and suffocating. But part of me also wonders if we should be pushing "beauty" as a standard at all. When I heard about a young woman named Nadia Ilse, a fourteen-year-old who got thousands of dollars in plastic surgery donated to her because she was bullied for her looks (which were perfectly fine),

I couldn't help but think that we never seem to question the idea that feeling beautiful is a worthy goal in the first place. I wrote then, and I still believe: "We should tell girls the truth: 'Beautiful' is bullshit, a standard created to make women into good consumers, too busy wallowing in self-loathing to notice that we're second-class citizens."

Ugly is powerful. Nothing has quite the same sting. Especially for the ladies. None of us want to be ugly; in fact, we all would really like to be beautiful—and it's killing us. Literally.

Whether we're puking or not eating or cutting ourselves (or letting doctors do it), young women are at the center of the beauty cult. We run that shit. But when people talk about young women having eating disorders or getting plastic surgery, they often assume that we don't know the consequences—health or otherwise. The sad truth is, young women do know. We just don't care.

I had a friend who struggled with bulimia for years. She went the therapy route, checked herself into a clinic—all the stuff you're supposed to do to get better. But she kept on bingeing and purging. When I asked her about it, she told me she *knew* this was unhealthy, she *knew* that this disease would likely kill her. But she didn't care. She said, "I would rather live a shorter life as a skinny girl than a full life being fat." That's how powerful ugly is.

I liken it to wearing amazing high-heel shoes. They're gorgeous, you know they make your legs look "better," and you rock them everywhere you go. Never mind that they're eating away at your feet and causing blisters that would make grown men faint. You suffer for beauty—or what beauty is supposed to be. We all do it in our own ways. And it's fucking up a lot more than our feet.

Unrealistic beauty standards and the lengths we go to reach them are pretty personal for me. Like I've said before (damn you, Doug MacIntyre), I remember how utterly and completely

In 2006, the FDA lifted the ban on silicone breast implants after a fourteen-year hiatus. Feminist organizations like NOW say that the implants have proven dangerous and that money and politics trumped women's health in the decision.

miserable it is to hate the way you look. I'm not talking about just wishing you were better looking, but about absolutely *hating* yourself because of your appearance. And I remember what it's like to be tortured because of it. When you're taught that the majority of your worth is in how aesthetically pleasing you are to boys—and then boys tell you you're ugly—there's something soul-crushing about that. Recently, I came across my junior high school diary, and it was fucking heartbreaking.

I'm so ugly I can't stand it. I have a big gross nose, pimples, hairy arms. I will never have a boy like me or a boyfriend. All of my friends are pretty and I will be the one with no one.

Mighty embarrassing, I know. Shockingly, boys did like me, and I did have a boyfriend eventually. But at the time I was sure I would go through life unloved because of what a nasty hag I was.

It's been a long time since grade school, and these days I think I'm looking pretty damn good. But as feminist, secure, and confident as I am now, any time someone makes a comment about my "Italian nose" or some such thing that recalls old complexes, I'm right back where I was in junior high. I can admit it. Sometimes I think that feeling will never go away. But recognizing where it came from, why I felt so shitty about myself, made a big difference. Especially when I found out that the ways in which our society keeps women obsessed with their looks serve a gross sexist purpose. In the same way that we're brought up by the media and influenced by cultural standards to think about men, relationships, and weddings constantly, we're taught to be forever worried about our appearance. It's a distraction, really. Just like a lot of the other shit I've been talking about. The more we're worked up about how fat we are or how hot we want to be, the less we're worried about the things that really matter, the things that will affect our lives.

Appearance as a Shut-the-Fuck-Up Tool

Nothing makes a gal clam up faster than someone telling her she's ugly. Or telling her that the way she looks/dresses/ appears has some bearing on who she is as a person.

Another little anecdote: In 2006, I was invited to meet former President Clinton (!) with a bunch of other bloggers. I was all revved up and feeling pretty honored. My mom cried when I told her—seriously. For a little Italian girl from

Queens whose parents didn't go to college, this shit was a big deal. And while I'm a feminist, I'm also a bit of a fashionista, so naturally, what to wear was on my mind. After much thought, I settled on a cap-sleeve crewneck sweater and black pants. I thought I looked pretty good. But, always the stickler, I remember asking my friend Bill that morning—who was also attending the lunch—if he thought the outfit was appropriate. Thumbs up.

So you can imagine my surprise when, mere days after the event, certain websites and blogs started to comment about the way I looked in a group photo that was taken at the end of the meeting. Some commenters on websites remarked that I looked hot; some said I was ugly. Many made quips about my being an "intern." Yeah, in reference to Monica Lewinsky. I guess having dark hair and being young in Clinton's presence automatically makes you fodder for tasteless jokes.

There was one site in particular—Althouse[1]—where the comments got particularly nasty. Never being a girl to just take someone's shit (I'm from Queens, remember?), I posted a sarcastic comment on the site, noting how lovely it was that women weren't being judged for their looks anymore. And then the shitstorm began. You see, the law professor running the website, Ann Althouse, wasn't too pleased that I had the nerve to speak up. She told me that it did appear as if I were "posing" (for a picture? Imagine!) and should therefore expect all sorts of nasty comments. Althouse then went on to write a whole new post called—you're going to love this—"Let's take a closer look at those breasts," in which she accused me of "breastblogging."

Because Feministing's logo is an ironic mudflap girl giving the finger, and our ad for shirts is worn by a woman with—gasp!—breasts, it turns out that I'm all tits, all the time.

> ❋ Apparently, Jessica writes one of those blogs that are all about using breasts for extra attention. Then, when she goes to meet Clinton, she wears a tight knit top that draws attention to her breasts and stands right in front of him and positions herself to make her breasts as obvious as possible?

What?! My modest crewneck sweater? I was shoving my tits in his face? It was all too much. You would think from the way she described it that I was pushing my boobs together while doing a pole dance in front of Clinton, instead of just, well, standing there.

And thus "Boobgate" began: hundreds of comments—some calling out said law professor on her bullshit; some calling me a whore and a hypocrite; more than one hundred thousand views of the notorious photo on my Flickr photo page; hundreds of links on both the left and right sides of the blogosphere; even a podcast claiming that the only reason I was invited to the blogger lunch was to be set up with Clinton. Seriously. And those are just the responses I'm aware of; I stopped checking after a couple of days. It was an online extravaganza, and for a weekend I had the most popular boobs in the blog world. And it wasn't fun.

At the end of the whole nasty mess, I realized something—or at least realized it more acutely. If you're a younger woman, no matter how much work you do, some-one is always going to claim that your success is due to the way you look or your general fuckability.

The fact that some folks couldn't fathom that I would be invited to this lunch for anything other than my appear-ance and potential whorishness is pretty depressing, but not shocking. Young women are constantly reminded that their only real worth is their ability to be ogled or ridiculed. That's what we're there for, silly! All of these nasty comments about my appearance and chest were there to remind me to shut the fuck up and know my place—which definitely wasn't, in their opinion, at lunch with a world leader.

So anyway, just wanted to point out that we're all subject to this kind of bullshit all the time. And even if we work hard, do "serious" political work, and do our best to sport cute crewneck sweaters, someone is always going to be hating.

But, of course, using looks as a method of silencing women isn't limited to young women. Pretty much any woman who speaks her mind (think politicians, journalists, feminists) is fair game for the shut-up-you-ugly-bitch line of argument. Or the you're-too-pretty-to-be-smart argument. I've been privy to both, and they both suck.

Some digital cameras now offer a "slimming" feature. Instant eating disorder!

I remember back when Clinton was president, everyone gave Hillary shit for her headbands and hairstyles. Headbands! The media even ragged on his daughter for not being pretty enough when she was a teenager (like that age isn't hard enough!). Disgusting.

And dear lord, how much time is spent in the media discussing Katie Couric's looks? Or any other public professional woman? If she's cute by beauty norms, then you can't take her seriously—or she's vain. If she's not, then she doesn't deserve to be in the public eye. The only solution? Nip and tuck, baby.

Don't Like It? Cut It Off.

Because of my already-mentioned issue with my nose, I used to beg—beg!—my parents to let me get a nose job. They were cruel, I argued, to let me walk around with this monstrosity on my face. Of course, I'm forever grateful that they wouldn't even entertain the notion of letting me get plastic surgery. But at the time I thought they were the worst.

There's something insanely sick about plastic surgery when you really think about it. Now, yes, I know—some people truly need corrective surgery or reconstruction. For some people who are trans, plastic surgery may be incredibly important. I'm aware. But don't go telling me that anyone "needs" silicone gel thingies shoved in their boobs for beauty's sake. No one needs that.

I mean, they are: Cutting. Open. Your. Body. And you're letting them. And paying them. I don't know. . . . There is just something about that that defies logic.

And it's become so normalized! Oh, don't like your tits? Shove some new ones in there! Hate your nose? Cut it off. Feeling chubby? Suck that fat out! You don't actually *want* that vagina, do you? Trim trim. (More on this one a little later, 'cause it's the one that makes the least sense to me.)

There's a quick fix for everything—if you have the money. The rich (whom we're supposed to look up to, I guess) get plastic surgery, so that makes it glamorous and desirable. Rather than vapid and wasteful. Which, let's be honest—it is.

Not only is this obsession with plastic surgery totally superficial, but it also presupposes that we're all sick or broken and in need of fixing. Seriously, have you seen *The Swan?* Perhaps the most horrifying (and yet transfixing) of reality shows, *The Swan* finds the "ugliest" people (women) around and "fixes" them. They're swept out of their homes and go into seclusion for months for extreme surgery on pretty much every part of their faces and bodies. But not before they get the victim's, I mean winner's, family and loved ones to talk on camera about how horrid-looking she is. You know, for dramatic effect.

There were a couple of things I found interesting about this show. One was the rhetoric of brokenness behind it. As if these women weren't getting plastic surgery to adhere to a beauty standard, but to fix something that was wrong with them. The doctors used deliberately "nice" language, like making your nose "match" your chin. Or getting rid of "excess" fat. How can it be excess if it's on you? It's not like someone stapled it on there and these doctors are there to make you "yourself" again.

There was also a lot of "life coaching," which was laughable, going on on *The Swan*. One of the show's producers—nipped and tucked to the extreme herself—called herself a life coach and would have one-on-one sessions with the potential Swans. I think this was partly to keep up the facade that somehow the makers of *The Swan* actually gave a shit about the women, but also to put out the message that being beautiful will cure your problems. And as nice a thought as this is, come on now. If your husband is cheating on you, it doesn't mean that you need to get prettier—it means he's a scumbag.

In a way, *The Swan* is totally telling about how we're supposed to view beauty and appearances. We're supposed to pity (and quietly mock) those who don't fit into the narrow standards of what beautiful is, and we're supposed to applaud them when they finally "fix" themselves (that's if you consider pulled-back skin and big, scary white teeth an improvement).

In real life, it's similar. If you're not constantly trying to "improve" yourself, even in the smallest ways (think waxing, tanning, manicures), you're gross and you don't "take care of" yourself. Just saying.

And unfortunately, these quick fixes are starting earlier and earlier for women. In 2003, more than 331,000 plastic

The *Los Angeles Times* reported in 2005 that Asian American women are increasingly seeking out skin-bleaching creams and medical procedures.

surgery procedures were performed on people younger than eighteen years old.

And you don't have to look very far in youth pop culture (I'm talking to you, MTV) to see how acceptable it's becoming for young people to get plastic surgery. On the MTV show *I Want a Famous Face*, young people get radical plastic surgery to look like their favorite celebrity, or, in the case of one girl, like a *Playboy* model. Sigh. But of course, the sexualization of beauty standards has been a long time coming. And it starts below the waist.

Beauty Standards . . . for Your Vagina

Oh, how I wish I were joking on this one. As if it's not bad enough that we have to get the hair ripped out of our sensitive lady parts so as to not offend the porn-raised boys of today, now we have to trim up our skin as well. Puke.

I don't know if it's the porn culture or the weird virginity-fetish stuff that's going on politically, but for some reason, "vaginal rejuvenation" surgery (as if it were tired or something) is superpopular. In Africa, they call it female genital mutilation, but in the United States, we call them designer vaginas. 'Cause we're civilized like that.

Vaginal rejuvenation surgery can mean a labia trim, liposuction on your outer lips, vaginal tightening, or even hymen "replacement." How many times did you just say *ouch* in your head? All so we can have "normal," "attractive" genitalia. You know, like in porn, where everyone has teeny-tiny vaginas with no hair.

What really pisses me off about this surgery is that it's being promoted using feminist language. Seriously. A press release for the Laser Vaginal Rejuvenation Institute reads, "Women now have equal sexuality rights!" It continues, "Today women are exercising their rights to sexual equality due to innovative vaginal surgeries."[2] Equality? Rights?

See, gals, it's *empowering* to cut pieces of your labia off! All the self-respecting girls are doing it.

But please, ladies, seriously. I know the love-your-vagina thing is a bit of a feminist cliché. So you know what? I don't care if you love it. But just do me a favor and don't cut it up. What did she ever do to you?

Buying Beauty

Of course, all the plastic surgery nonsense isn't just about enforcing beauty standards—it's about making money. As is most everything related to making you feel shitty about your appearance. Every makeup commercial or skin cream ad (or diet pill ad, and so on) has a specific purpose: to make you spend your money.

Consumerism is at the heart of beauty standards. After all, who's telling you what's (and who's) hot? Fashion mags, for example, survive by selling ads, ads that tell you your skin will be disgusting if you don't buy the latest microderm scrubbing bubbling foamy face wash. They all depend on your feeling ugly.

Because guess what? If you think your looks are just fine and dandy as they are, you're not going to buy face creams and makeup and diet pills. You're just going to hang out, feeling great and doing productive things. But if you feel ugly and fat, you're going to spend as much money as possible to make sure you're doing all you can to be pretty.

I mean, if you really start to think about the money you spend on the way you look, it's scary. The makeup, clothes, products (hair, body, et cetera), waxing, tanning, manicures, facials, plastic surgery—it's never-ending.

Or maybe you don't fall for any of that bullshit. Good for you. Me, I'll always have an affinity for facials and vintage purses. I can admit my weaknesses. But I'm secure in knowing where the desire for these things comes from—and that I don't need them to feel good about myself.

It's important to remember why some folks *need* us to feel ugly. It serves a specific purpose: to make us spend, to distract us, and ultimately to make us disappear.

Food? Who Needs Food?

There's something about eating disorders that is simultaneously disgusting and fascinating to the American public. We tsk-tsk about how young women are starving themselves or bingeing and purging, but at the end of the day, we're still buying magazines with skeletal, sick-looking actresses on the covers (and you know exactly the ladies I'm talking about).

We love to hate them. We love to pity them. But when was the last time you saw an article headline that read, "Dear Lord, Someone Get This Girl a Doctor, Seriously!"? I find it more than a little disturbing that we're watching these actresses and models literally die—we really are—and we're not doing anything about it.

Is it because we secretly hate them? Because we don't care? I don't know. But it's fucked.

You know what else is screwed up? Eating disorders have the highest death rate of any mental illness. We really are killing ourselves. Of course, eating disorders aren't all a consequence of socially enforced beauty standards. Some say it's genetic, some say it's dependent on personality type, some say it's the family you're raised in. I'm sure it's all of these things.

I'm also a firm believer (and I'm not a doctor, so this is just my humble opinion) that the diet culture we live in is also to blame. I mean, how much calorie-counting can a gal take before she goes apeshit?

One summer, my sister lost a ton of weight. Too much. She did not look good—she looked sick. The truly upsetting part was that when she lost this weight, a lot of our family

A 2005 study from New York University says that the more a woman weighs, the less her family income and occupational prestige.

and friends started remarking how great she looked. They congratulated her, told her how super it was that she was losing weight. I wanted to throttle them.

Vanessa finally caught on that she wasn't well. I remember her looking at pictures of herself from that summer—I think it was the first time she really saw how she looked from the outside. She said, "Damn, I look too skinny." And that was it for her and her obsessive dieting. Obviously, this isn't the case for most women.

In fact, a recent study found that more than 80 percent of college women diet—no matter how much they weigh. And the *Journal of the American Academy of Child and Adolescent Psychiatry* says that 40 percent of nine-year-old girls have dieted, and that girls as young as five are concerned about dieting. I'll repeat that: Five-year-olds are worried about their weight.

There's something seriously amiss when women are spending so much of their time and energy, you know, killing themselves than they are actually living their lives.

So please, gals. Eat something.

And yes, men have body standards to live up to as well. I know this. But their body standards—big, strong, muscular—push them to be strong, to take up space. Ours—skinny, skeletal, weak—push us to be fragile, to take up less space, to disappear essentially. I'd say those are some vastly different expectations.

So What Now?

So, yeah. Shit is fucked up when it comes to appearances and women. We're expected to be hot—but if we are, we're vain and stupid. And if we're not hot, we're useless. Kind of hard to get around.

But we're not stupid. We *know* that we're doing damage to ourselves—not only to our bodies but also to our mental well-being. And it's not worth it. It's not worth the pain. It's not worth the time and the money. And really—with all the money or time you spend in front of the mirror—have you yet to be truly happy? I'm guessing not.

So what can we do?

Thankfully, some people are taking unhealthy beauty standards seriously.

During fall 2006 Fashion Week, Spain banned too-skinny models from a Madrid fashion show,[3] and the mayor of Milan, Italy, said that she would seek a similar ban for her city's fashion shows.[4] Around the same time, designer Jean-Paul Gaultier used a size 20 model in his fashion show as a comment on the skinny-model debate.[5]

Another interesting turn of events has been the Dove "real beauty" ads—which feature . . . real women. (Too bad they're selling cellulite cream with the "real" women!)

Now, clearly, these are just small steps—and they're still mired in consumerism, so it's hard to take them seriously. So we're not going to be changing the world of beauty expectations anytime soon.

But we can do one thing that, while totally simple, is completely revolutionary: We can stop hating ourselves so much. I know sometimes that's much easier said than done, but we have to try. I mean, really. In a world that makes it near impossible to feel up to par, liking yourself and the way you look is a revolutionary act. I'm so self-help, I know; I'm aware it's a bit cheesy. But that doesn't make it any less true.

A woman's place
is in the house.
And the Senate.

12

SEX AND THE CITY VOTERS, MY ASS

It's kind of sad that women are considered a "special" voting demographic, but such is life—that's what happens when white men are considered the default, the "real" voters. But this focus on women as voters actually helped feminist values tremendously in the 2012 presidential election. Thanks to a long line of Republicans saying ridiculous things about women, abortion, or rape—combined with the increased amount of legislation centered on rolling back women's reproductive rights—the focus on women's votes was intense. Obama's campaign used this to their advantage, hammering Mitt Romney on his lack of support for women's issues. Republicans, however, dismissed women out of hand, continually saying they didn't believe that women cared about issues like birth control or abortion. This was a huge mistake. The gender gap ended up being 18 percent—much higher than the twelve-point gap in the 2008 election. Women also made up a majority of the electorate, and unmarried women were

23 percent of voters. So politicians beware! That said, we need to flex our political muscle beyond the voting booth—and we need to ensure that our issues are addressed not just in election campaigns, but in policy and culture as well.

Ah, politics. We love to hate it.

Women are underrepresented participation- and representation-wise in politics, and it's a damn shame. We're getting fucked over constantly through anti-woman legislation, and yet we're not running for office and we're voting at abysmal rates.

Younger women in particular are being assailed for not picking up the political slack—and you know what? This time it may be warranted. While younger women are definitely active in a lot of ways, it seems that electoral politics just doesn't take precedence in our lives. And it should.

I'm a big believer in social-justice activism, and I get as frustrated with U.S. politics as the next gal, but if we're not going to get involved, we're in trouble.

So why are young women so loath to get involved?

My own opinion is that young women especially are steered away from all things political from such a young age that by the time they get around to adulthood, they're freaked out and intimidated by the process.

Plus, women are pretty consistently told that they don't know what they're talking about, and their opinions are often dismissed. Add to that a general self-consciousness about all things political, and we have a problem. But of course, this is just my little theory.

There's also the fact that many young women don't feel like politicians speak to them and the issues that matter to them—we're talked about more than we're talked to. But we can't expect lasting change on behalf of women's rights without political action.

So it's really just time to suck it up.

Numbers Don't Lie

Despite gains made through the years, women still only make up 15 percent of the seats in Congress, 14 percent of the one hundred seats in the Senate, and 15 percent of the 435 seats in the House of Representatives. And of those eighty-one women serving on Congress in 2006, only 24 percent of them are women of color.

In state executive positions, like governor and lieutenant governor, women make up 24 percent of available positions.[1] And we're not making much progress, either. A report from the Center for Women in Government & Civil Society at the University at Albany found that from 1998 to 2005, the percentage of women in state government leadership positions only rose from 23.1 to 24.7. Not very impressive.[2]

So on all counts, we're not even close to equal.

But it's not just political representation that's poor for women in the United States—it's participation as well. Apparently, we're not big on voting.

According to Women's Voices. Women Vote., fifteen million unmarried women were not registered to vote in 2004 and almost twenty million unmarried women didn't vote in

2004; if unmarried women had voted at the same rate as married women, there would have been more than six million more voters at the polls[3] (and maybe we wouldn't be stuck with Bushie right now!). If you're married, I'm not trying to leave you out of the equation—I just think it's interesting that so many younger women (we tend to be the unmarried ones) aren't participating in politics. It's fucking terrible, really.

The Headband Treatment

Remember the headband treatment of Hillary I mentioned? Well, that's pretty much par for the course when it comes to women politicians.

While all women are subject to being judged by their appearance, women in leadership positions get it like crazy. There's something about a woman in power that makes people feel like they need to put her in "her place."

Take this story, for example. Former governor of Maryland and current (as of 2006) State Comptroller William Donald Schaefer told a *Washington Post* reporter that his 2006 opponent, Janet Owens, is a "prissy little miss" who wears "long dresses [and] looks like Mother Hubbard—it's sort of like she was a man." He said in an interview, "She's got these long clothes on and an old-fashioned hairdo. . . . You know, it sort of makes you real mad."[4] Uh huh. Can you imagine someone talking about the hairdo and clothes of a male candidate? Yeah, not gonna happen. By the way, Schaefer is kind of a known douchebag. He harassed a twenty-four-year-old administrative aide by watching her

Leading up to the 2004 presidential election, a company called Axis of Eve created political panties to encourage voting among young women. The slogans included "Give Bush the Finger" and "My Cherry for Kerry."

ass as she brought over a cup of tea and instructed her to "walk again." (He later said that "this little girl" should be "happy that I observed her going out the door.")[5] Ah, sexist politicians.

And judging women politicians on their looks isn't limited to their opponents—who clearly have something to gain by going on the attack. The media does it as well. The White House Project (www.thewhitehouseproject.org), a nonprofit dedicated to getting more women in politics, did a study researching the media coverage of Elizabeth Dole's presidential campaign compared with that of then–Texas Governor George W. Bush, Arizona Senator John McCain, and publisher Steve Forbes; they examined 462 articles and what they found wasn't pretty.

Dole, shockingly, received more "personal" coverage (comments about her personality and the way she dressed) than any of the male candidates. Thirty-five percent of the paragraphs on Dole were personal, compared to 27 percent for Bush, 22 percent for McCain, and 16.5 percent for Forbes.[6]

Shit, even when *The New York Times* covered a dinner honoring women in the government, they ran it in the "Styles" section with a pink purse graphic!

Some women have found, well, interesting ways to fight back. One 2006 Alabama gubernatorial candidate, Loretta Nall, was pissed when a local newspaper ran a picture of her cleavage and went on to comment on her breasts. So Nall countered (quite sassily, I might add), "I don't approve of political reporters who are titillated by my breasts while ignoring the serious issues which affect a whole lot of poor and disenfranchised Alabamians,"[7] and went on to create a new campaign slogan: "More of these boobs [hers] and less of these boobs [incumbent politicians]!!" Hysterical.

But of course, it's not just appearance that women politicians are attacked for. It's their personalities. The most common insults? "Ballbuster," "bitch," and the like. Because clearly, all women who work in politics are "unfeminine" and annoying. Never mind that perseverance and an ability to get shit done are generally thought of as *good* qualities in male politicians. But as a woman, you can't win. 'Cause if you're not a "bitch," you're too "soft" for politics.

Conservative columnist John Podhoretz actually tried to argue on Fox News that calling Hillary Clinton a bitch in his book *Can She Be Stopped?* was actually a compliment. You know, because it means she's like a guy.

> ❀ I use the B-word to describe her and say that that is a virtue as the first woman presidential, you know, possibility. . . . The first woman president has to be somebody who has qualities that we commonly associate with being unfeminine.[8]

Right, 'cause feminine and, you know, someone who is a woman would be unfit for the presidency.

By the way, he also called her "flat" and "unwomanly."[9] Sweet.

This kind of sexist stereotyping about who is fit for power is pretty (depressingly) common. Sometimes folks even try to use "positive" stereotypes.

A 2006 *New York Times* article reported that the Democratic party was looking to run women candidates as outsiders against a "culture of corruption." Because women are never corrupt, apparently.

Representative Rahm Emanuel of Illinois, the chairman of the Democratic Congressional Campaign Committee, said in the piece, "In an environment where people are disgusted with politics in general, who represents clean and change? Women."[10] We're so pure and good and all. Barf.

What's truly sad is that women candidates probably *do* have a better chance of winning elections based on what people think of their personal lives over their actual politics. As my coblogger Ann Friedman wrote about the article, "The public loves women politicians whose personal lives adhere to the stereotypes (devoted wife, mother, etc.), but has a much harder time stomaching women whose political positions are actually pro-woman."[11] No joke.

But that's not to say that women aren't kicking ass when they are in political office.

Some Great Women Politicians

Okay, getting more women in office is definitely important. But not just anyone. Let's get some pro-women women in there.

SOME COOL STUFF THAT WOMEN POLITICIANS HAVE DONE:

New York Representative Carolyn Maloney introduced legislation that would regulate the advertisement of "crisis pregnancy centers" that aim to convince pregnant women against having abortions.[12]

Democratic Senators Patty Murray of Washington and Hillary Clinton of New York blocked the confirmation of Bush nominee Andrew von Eschenbach to head the FDA until the agency stepped up and made emergency contraception available over the counter.[13]

In 2005, Kansas Governor Kathleen Sebelius vetoed a bill that would have required state abortion clinics to adopt more rigorous guidelines, saying she won't get behind legislative action that singles out abortion.[14]

Maxine Waters, in addition to having an awesome record on women's rights, cofounded the Los Angeles–based organization the Black Women's Forum.[15]

SOME COOL STUFF WOMEN POLITICIANS HAVE SAID:

Former Texas Governor Ann Richards: "Ginger Rogers did everything Fred Astaire did. She just did it backwards and in high heels."[16]

Former Congresswoman Bella Abzug: "We are coming down from our pedestal and up from the laundry room. We want an equal share in government and we mean to get it."[17]

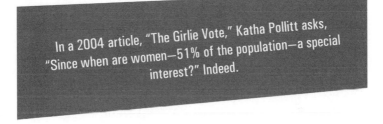

In a 2004 article, "The Girlie Vote," Katha Pollitt asks, "Since when are women—51% of the population—a special interest?" Indeed.

Former Congresswoman Pat Schroeder: "When people ask me why I am running as a woman, I always answer, 'What choice do I have?'"[18]

But don't get me wrong. I'm not saying that we should be electing women just by virtue of their having ovaries. Women politicians have definitely been known to fuck over other women.

Democratic Louisiana Governor Kathleen Blanco, for example, signed a sweeping abortion ban in her state that made all abortion illegal—even in cases of rape and incest. Not cool.

The important thing is that we're participating—whether it's by running, voting, or supporting (financially or otherwise) candidates who make a difference for women. Don't leave shit up to others, 'cause that's how we get fucked over.

The Difference Young Women Make

The 2004 presidential elections were all about women, in a way. We were told "it's up to the women"[19] to make sure that George W. Bush wasn't reelected.

Single women were all the rage during that election—yet, of course, they called us *Sex and the City* voters. Charming. And not at all condescending. (It kills me that even when we have potential power, the media chose to pretty much dismiss us with that name.)

You see, back in 2004, polls showed that single women favored Kerry over Bush by almost 26 percent, while married women preferred Bush.[20] But unfortunately, twenty million unmarried women didn't vote. This isn't to say we fucked up the election—after all, the Supreme Court picked the president, not us—but it goes to show you the power we had that we *just didn't use*.

And why in the world not? Chris Desser, codirector of Women's Voices. Women Vote., said in 2004 that "one-third of unmarried women polled said their main reason for not voting is that they believe their lives will not improve, no matter who is elected."[21]

Kind of sad, but I can see where that trepidation comes from. What have politicians done for us lately, really? Sure, they'll throw us a bone on repro rights every once in a while, and I definitely love me some VAWA, but it's hard to feel connected to a political system that generally pays you no mind.

But the thing is, we can't let the fact that politicians don't care about us (for the most part) translate into our not car-

2004 was the first election in which women voted at a higher rate than men in the U.S. presidential election.

ing about politics. It's just too damned important. Because it's really fucked up that laws affecting our lives, at the most personal levels, are being decided overwhelmingly by men.

When Bush signed the "partial birth" ban into effect, someone took a snapshot of him and all the supporting politicians as they hovered around him while he essentially signed away our rights. Guess what? The picture spoke a thousand words—it was all men. Now that's fucked up.

This isn't to say that male politicians can't be allies in women's rights—Representative Henry Waxman has put out reports on fake abortion clinics and exposed abstinence-only education as ineffective and dangerous; Senator Joe Biden was one of the original authors of VAWA.

I just think that there's something particularly ironic about men legislating our rights away—and we've got to stop letting it happen.

What Other Countries Do

When I was in grad school, I interned at a great international women's organization called the Women's Environment & Development Organization (WEDO), where I would later go on to work full-time. While there, I worked on a campaign in its Gender and Governance program called the 50/50 Campaign.[22] The campaign seeks to increase women's representation and participation in all decision-making processes worldwide, with an emphasis on national parliaments.

WEDO reached out to women on local and regional levels, and almost three hundred organizations and eighteen national and regional campaigns were launched. The priorities of the campaign include "political party reform, which includes adopting gender balance strategies" and campaign finance reform.[23]

Basically, the idea is that most campaign finance systems favor incumbents—and since most incumbents are men . . . well, you get the idea. The political party reform is a bit more controversial. The 50/50 campaign advocates establishing quotas as a way to increase women's representation in decision-making positions.

So this means that a certain percentage of candidate or political office seats are reserved for women. Controversial? Yes, definitely. Americans don't like the word "quotas," that's for sure. But it's proven way effective. All countries achieved critical mass (30 percent) of women politicians after implementing party or legal quotas.

Party quotas are voluntary; political parties guarantee that a certain percentage of women will be selected as election candidates. Political parties in Austria, Finland, Germany, Iceland, Mozambique, Norway, Sweden, and South Africa use this system.

Legal quotas make it mandatory for political parties to set aside a certain percentage of parliamentary seats for women. If parties don't comply, they can be disqualified from the election or have government campaign funding withdrawn. Legal quotas are used in Argentina, Belgium, Costa Rica, France, and Rwanda.[24]

I don't think the United States will be implementing quotas anytime soon—and I don't even know if this is the answer for us—but I wanted to put it out there.

The thing is, the idea behind achieving a critical mass of women in political decision-making positions comes from the idea that there is policy change when there are more women in politics. Some say that this is that kind of "good" sexism: like, women are not corrupt, or we're cooler on issues affecting other women. It kind of presupposes that just by having vaginas, we're going to make good policy decisions. Kind of makes me uncomfortable.

Patsy Mink was the first Asian American woman elected to the U.S. House of Representatives in 1064; in 1908, Shirley Chisholm was the first African American woman to be elected.

But that said, there seems to be *some* truth to this line of thought. Countries with the highest percentages of women in politics tend to have great policies affecting women's lives.

Sweden, for example, which has one of the highest percentages of women in political office in the world, has amazing policies for women: Because of employment laws, women's salaries are, on average, 90 percent of men's,[25] and the country has an amazing public childcare system.[26]

But then again, who's to say that's not because the government is more progressive as a whole? It's debatable—so seriously, look into these things and figure out what you think for yourself.

Stop Futzing Around

So the moral of the story is that yes, sometimes politics truly can suck for women (voters and politicians). But that doesn't mean we can just wash our hands of the whole thing.

Women can create change on all sorts of levels (my favorite being straight-up activism), but electoral politics is something we *must* be involved in. So get your shit together and start figuring out what you're going to do about it.

A great place to start is the White House Project. Not only does it have fantastic resources, but it also runs campaigns designed to get more women to run for political office.

Its Vote, Run, Lead campaign is particularly cool. The project aims to get younger women involved in the political process through training, media campaigns, and grassroots organizing. There are additional resources in the resource guide, but you get the idea. It's time that young women took some initiative; we have to stop letting other people talk for us and about us (and calling us *Sex and the City* voters!). So let's speak for ourselves.

So many –isms,
so little time

13

A QUICK ACADEMIC ASIDE

There is perhaps no idea more important in feminism than intersectionality. It's also the most debated, talked about, and struggled with concept in the movement. Nothing makes me happier, though, than seeing the way that intersectionality—the idea and the practice—has become such a central part of the work feminists do online. Like with all feminist issues, though, practicing intersectionality is not something that is just done and then you don't need to worry about—it's a constantly moving thing, something that shifts and changes and needs to be thought about and utilized every day and with every feminist act. Sometimes we'll fail at it—I certainly do. But the important thing is that we continue to see it as the theory that holds feminism together—and the activism that will ensure justice all around, not just for a few. As one

233

my favorite feminists Flavia Dzodan has famously said, "My feminism will be intersectional or it will bullshit!"

I'm not a big fan of waxing academic, which is why most of the chapters in this book are informal (and, I know, slightly potty-mouthed). But if there's one thing—something ridiculously important—that can't be missed, it's this.

Some folks call it intersectionality; others call it multiple oppressions; some call it the intersection of oppressions. Whatever you call it, the point is that different kinds of "-isms" (sexism, classism, racism) all intersect in a truly fucked-up way. Yeah, academic or not, my cursing just won't quit.

There used to be a whole bunch of infighting among feminists—I guess there still is, to some extent—about this idea of sisterhood, that we're all in the same boat sexism-wise. Because no matter how different we are, or how different our experiences may be, we're all oppressed as women, right?

Not so much. This idea of common oppression among all women almost always negates the lived experiences of actual women—because we don't all experience sexism in the same way. Classism, racism, ageism, homophobia—you name it—all come into play in the ways sexism is acted out against women. And while the idea of sisterhood is nice, a sisterhood that's built on the idea that we're all oppressed in the same way tends to erase things like race, class, and sexual orientation. Because, unfortunately, when feminism is talked about, it's still positioned from the experience of a white, middle- to upper-class, hetero gal. It just is. And if that's the only way we think of feminism, then we're essentially erasing the existence of any other woman who doesn't function within those confines. Yeah, not so cool.

Audre Lorde (whom I had a massive academic crush on in college) wrote a lot of great stuff concerning the intersection of oppressions, but my fave essay of hers by far on this topic is "Age, Race, Class, and Sex."

> ☀ Certainly there are very real differences between us of race, age, and sex. But it is not those differences between us that are separating us. It is rather our refusal to recognize those differences, and to examine the distortions which result from our misnaming them and their effects upon human behavior and expectation.[1]

So, ignoring the differences between women—whatever they may be—is hindering the women's movement. Terribly.

In comes the idea of intersectionality as a tool to discuss and create change within feminism and feminist activism. The cool thing is, this idea of intersectionality isn't just an abstract idea in academic feminism—it *is* being used in a real way. In the work that's done by the United Nations on behalf of women, for example, the intersection of oppressions is often talked about:

> ☀ Central to the realization of the human rights of women is an understanding that women do not experience discrimination and other forms of human rights violations solely on the grounds of gender, but for a multiplicity of reasons, including ages, dis-

ability, health status, race, ethnicity, caste, class, national origin, and sexual orientation. Various bodies and entities within the UN have to a certain extent recognized the intersectionality of discrimination in women's lives.[2]

The idea of intersectional oppressions was even used in the Beijing Platform for Action and other documents related to the UN's Fourth World Conference on Women. (Translation: That's a big deal.)

Just a few "-isms" that need to be in our heads whenever we're thinking about feminism:

RACISM

Women of color shouldn't be expected to separate out their oppressions: *Well, let's see, was he judging me because I am a woman, or because I am a black woman?* There's no way to do that, to separate out your gender and race in your lived experience. But the idea of universal sisterhood in oppression almost necessitates that—from a white perspective. That, my friends, is what we call some ill white privilege.

Peggy McIntosh has a widely used (in women's studies) piece on white privilege that you should read in its entirety if you ever have a chance. She talks about how, through feminism, she's seen men's unwillingness to admit that they are overprivileged, and then relates it to race:

❋ Thinking through unacknowledged male privilege as a phenomenon, I realized that, since hierarchies in our society are interlocking, there was most likely a phenomenon of white privilege that was similarly denied and protected. As a white person, I realized I had been taught about racism as something that puts others at a disadvantage, but had been taught not to see one of its corollary aspects, white privilege, which puts me at an advantage.[3]

McIntosh goes through a list of privileges that being white affords her. Just a few: I can turn on the television or open to the front page of the paper and see people of my race widely represented; I do not have to educate my children to be aware of systemic racism for their own daily physical protection; when I am told about our national heritage, or about "civilization," I am shown that people of my color made it what it is; I am not made acutely aware that my shape, bearing, or body odor will be taken as a reflection on my race; I can choose blemish cover-up or bandages in "flesh" color and have them more or less match my skin; I can easily buy posters, postcards, picture books, greeting cards, dolls, toys, and children's magazines featuring people of my race.

You get the point. It's insanely important that white feminists are acutely aware of their white privilege—in life and in feminism. It's not the responsibility of women of color to "teach" white feminists about their experiences. As Audre Lorde said (I told you I love her), "Whenever the need for some pretense of communication arises, those who profit from our oppression call upon us to share our knowledge with them. In other words, it is the responsibility of the oppressed to teach the oppressor their mistakes. . . . The oppressors maintain their position and evade responsibility. . . ."[4]

CLASSISM

I'll tell you a little story about something that made me acutely aware of classism—it was the craziest wake-up call ever. I went to a public high school in New York that tested students for entry (it was kind of a dorky math and science school). The majority of my friends in high school were gals from the Upper West Side of Manhattan. They had awesome apartments and college-educated parents who were professors, artists, judges, and so on. I grew up in Long Island City, Queens, which at the time was not considered the best neighborhood in the world. My parents grew up in Queens and Brooklyn, got married when they were still teenagers, and never went to college.

But hey, it was all good to me. My friends were my friends, and we were all the same. Then one day, after a couple of my girlfriends spent some time at my house after school, one of them remarked, "Your mom is so cute! Her accent sounds so . . . uneducated!" They all laughed. I don't think she meant it to be cruel, or even realized what she was saying. But after that moment, it was difficult to be around my high school friends. I had this overwhelming feeling of not belonging. I didn't know if they were laughing at my potty-mouthed jokes because I was funny, or because I was playing up to the Italian Queens girl stereotype. I wondered, when they told me they didn't like something I was wearing, whether it was because of a difference in taste, or because they thought I looked "trashy."

Later, in college (at a private Southern university—I lasted a year before transferring back to New York), I would try to tone down the behavior I thought marked me as "lower class." I tried to drop cursing so much, the Queens accent slowly disappeared, and I continued to hang out with kids who had gone to boarding schools and to pretend I knew what the hell "summering" was. But you can't pass for long. I would later realize that a lot of the hellishly sexist experiences I went through in college were completely tied up with classism. I was called a slut not only because I had the gall to sleep with a guy I was dating, but also because I dressed differently, talked differently (no matter how I tried to hide it), and was seen as the trashy Queens girl on scholarship. So I know this is a little more personal than academic, but hey—the personal is political, right?

HOMOPHOBIA/HETEROSEXISM

In the same way a woman of color can't divvy up her oppressions, neither can a gay woman—or a gay, black woman, for that matter. There isn't a "double oppression" or a "triple oppression"; it's just an intersection of oppressions that plays out differently in every woman's life.

By the way, I know the word "homophobia" is used a lot—but the term "heterosexism" isn't nearly as common. So, just a quick explanation: "Heterosexism creates the climate for homophobia with its assumption that the world is and must be heterosexual and its display of power and privilege as the norm."[5]

In other words, when you see couples in magazines or TV shows, they're almost always going to be straight. And if they're not straight, a big deal is made out of said couple's being gay. It's not just posited as the norm. When a gay couple kisses in the street, or holds hands, they're rubbing the gay in our faces, but when straight couples do it, it's cool. I'd say that heterosexism is far more insidious than homophobia—because it's more accepted.

Something on homophobia and hetereosexism that I always found interesting is how they're so ridiculously related to sexism. In Suzanne Pharr's essay "Homophobia: A Weapon of Sexism," she writes that when women are called dykes and lesbians, it is almost always because they are believed to have "crossed the line" in some way. Kinda why so many people label feminists as lesbians.

* To be a lesbian is to be perceived as someone who has stepped out of line, who has moved out of sexual/economic dependence on a male, who is woman-identified. A lesbian is perceived as someone who can live without a man, and who is therefore (however illogically) against men. A lesbian is perceived as being outside the acceptable, routinized order of things. . . . A lesbian is perceived as a threat to the nuclear family, to male dominance and control, to the very heart of sexism.[6]

So it's not really women loving women that irks people—it's that they're transgressing, refusing to conform to societal perceptions of what women are supposed to be.

Just something to think about.

And yes, I realize there are a ton more "-isms"—ableism or ageism, for example. The same ideas apply to those, and to any number of women's lived experiences. These are just the "-isms" I chose to focus on for now.

And now, bordering on obsession with Lorde, I'll leave you with a quote:

> ☀ Our future survival is predicated upon our ability to relate within equality. As women, we must rot our internalized patterns of oppression within ourselves if we are to move beyond the most superficial aspects of social change. Now we must recognize difference among women who are our equals, neither inferior nor superior, and devise ways to use each other's difference to enrich our visions and our joint struggles.

A feminist's
work is
never done

14

GET TO IT

What I love about updating this chapter is that I don't need
to say much about how to get active—because chances are,
you probably already know. There's a vibrant feminist movement online in a way there wasn't when *FFF* was first published that makes getting involved that much easier. But the
nuances of activism aren't always obvious. So I'm going to
give you advice I give to young people who ask me (and I
get asked this a lot) what the best way is for them to make a
difference.

Start local: You know better than I do the best way you
can make an impact in your own community. What's going on
in your school, in your town? I'm betting you already know
the best places to start. The other thing about starting small
is that you can see a more demonstrable impact on the community, which can be more rewarding than signing a petition

for a national cause (though you should that, too!). If you're interested in working for a feminist organization, consider working for a small, local one over a larger national group. You'll get more experience, be relied on more often, and be given more responsibility. Take care of yourself: Doing this work is exhausting physically, mentally, and emotionally. It's not something we can turn off at the end of the day and that takes a toll on people. Self-care can be a radical act—make sure to participate in it! Most important, though—remember that you are making a difference. Every time you call out a friend for telling a racist joke, every time you start a discussion about sexism in the media, every time you pass on a feminist article—these are all small forms of activism that create ripples of change.

So what the hell to do now, huh?

While realizing that feminism is, in fact, completely necessary can be an awesome (though scary) thing, figuring out what to do with that information isn't always clear.

I mean, it's easy to get depressed about all of these obstacles that women are facing. Because it *is* depressing. And while I've spent the majority of this book outlining some—not all—of the fucked-up issues affecting women, I want to flip the script a bit and focus on what we can actually do about it.

Clearly, some of these issues are enormous and aren't going to be solved anytime soon. Systematic oppression of women isn't going to just go away. But we can change our own worlds—and others', by proxy.

One of the best things about feminism, in my opinion, is that you don't have to be a professional feminist to take part in the movement. And feminism is something you can be involved in without dedicating your life to it. Granted, once you go feminist, it's hard to look at the world in the same way—and that does affect your whole life. But just because sexism is pretty overwhelming at times, it doesn't mean that taking action against it has to be.

So I figured I'd give you some ideas of where to start, focusing on the topics we've already talked about. Take them and run with them.

Sex

- ☀ Get educated. If your school or the school in your local area is teaching abstinence-only education, do something about it. Get involved in the school board. Start handing out condoms in school with information about comprehensive sex ed. Let other students know that you're getting the shit end of the stick education-wise. Enlist the support of empathetic parents. Don't let a generation of young people grow up thinking that condoms cause cancer and girls don't like sex!

- ☀ Fuck up the double standard. Don't let people call girls sluts! Engage folks in conversations about why they think it's cool for guys to hook up, but not girls.

- ☀ Be proud of yourself; never feel ashamed. Feeling proud of yourself and your sexual decisions in a world that tries to make you feel ashamed is a revolutionary act.

- If you're going to "go wild," think about why you want to. If it's honestly for your own pleasure and enjoyment, cool beans. If it's not . . . think some more. If your friends are flashing their tits for no better reason than a free shirt and some attention, talk to them about it.

- Take control of your sexuality. As I said in Chapter 2: Be safe, be smart, and don't take shit from anyone about the informed decisions you make.

- Have orgasms. By any means necessary. ☺

Pop Culture

- Don't believe the hype. Roll your eyes when you see a sexist ad and point out its bullshittery to everyone around you.

- Value yourself for what the media doesn't—your intelligence, your street smarts, your ability to play a kick-ass game of pool, whatever. So long as it's not just valuing yourself for your ability to look hot in a bikini and be available to men, it's an improvement.

- Call people out on their crap. If you see a shitty ad or a sexist commercial, write a letter to the folks who put out the product; tell your friends to do the same.

- Reject *Maxim, Playboy,* and any other form of pop culture that tells you you're not hot enough.

Start your own magazine that highlights what's really "hot" about women. Or, if you're lazy, just snarl in sexist mags' general direction.

☀ Nominate someone you know to the REAL Hot 100 (www.therealhot100.org), a campaign that's the antithesis of *Maxim*'s Hot 100 list. It features women who are hot for what they do, not how they look. Its tagline is "See how hot smart can be."

Reproductive Rights

☀ Take birth control. Trust me.

☀ Volunteer at your local clinic—whether as an escort, an intern, or whatever—show them your support! And help them raise money. I've been noticing that all the billboards I see that deal with the abortion issue are overwhelmingly anti-choice; that's because pro-choice orgs don't have the money to put ads out there—they're too busy providing women with care.

☀ Find out about your local pharmacies' policy on giving women their birth control and emergency contraception prescriptions. If they're trying to keep women from their legal right to birth control, throw a shit fit. Alert the media, write letters; if it's a chain pharmacy, make sure the pharmacist is adhering to the company standard. Make sure that women in your area won't have a hard time accessing their prescriptions.

☀ Be on the lookout for "organizations" in your state trying to push long-term birth control and sterilization on women. Make local media aware of their agenda and how it's intrinsically anti-woman.

◉ Find out about the parental notification/consent laws in your state and ask your local reproductive rights organization how you can help younger women in your area.

◉ Remember that anti-choicers, at the heart of it, are just folks who are horrified at the idea of pre-marital sex. They're not the arbiters of morality, just a bunch of folks who think girls should be forever virgins.

Violence

◉ Remember that there is no such thing as a rapeable offense. I don't care what you were wearing, how drunk you were, or how much hooking up you may have done beforehand. It's not your fault.

◉ Volunteer, volunteer, volunteer! There are plenty of rape crisis and domestic violence centers that need help—even a little bit. When I was a rape crisis counselor, I volunteered one night a month. Not a lot of time, but it makes a huge difference.

◉ If you talk to your friends about rape, bring up rape culture. Don't let violence against women be talked about as isolated, nonsystematic incidents.

◉ Don't stay with a person who hits you, emotionally abuses you, or threatens you in any way.

◉ Be safe, but remember that you shouldn't have to live your life by a rape schedule.

- Be proactive. Start an anti-violence group in your area—whether it's free rides home for local women or a counseling group or an awareness-raising class for men. Do something that appeals to you and helps women.

- Holla back. Like that blog I mentioned that has women take pictures of street harassers,[1] make men accountable for their public actions. Start your own holla back site!

Work and Money

- Do something fun for Equal Pay Day (usually the last Tuesday in April). One idea: Throw a party where men have to pay twenty-five cents more for drinks than women to bring attention to the wage gap.

- Call bullshit on opt-out articles—if your local media runs a piece on women "choosing" to stay home, contact them and let them know what you think.

- Start fighting for childcare now! Look to organizations like Family Initiative and Child Care Inc. for information and ways to get involved. It may seem early to start worrying about kids, but you don't want to be stuck with lousy childcare options if you decide to go the mommy route. And if you're not going to have kids, do it for the other women who will.

- Work your ass off. Doing what you love is fulfilling; work is fulfilling. And if staying at home and taking care of kids is something you can do and want to do, cool. But don't underestimate the pride and satisfaction that come with working at a job you love.

Dating and Beyond

- Pay for yourself. Just suck it up and do it.

- If you want to get married, cool. But think about the not-so-cool traditions associated with getting hitched: the ownership, the consumerism, the focus on glitz over love. If you're going to do it, do it for the marriage, not the ring.

- For the love of god, don't change your last name. At least do me a favor and hyphenate.

- Fight for the right for everyone to get married, 'cause it's hard to have fun when everyone can't join in. The Human Rights Campaign is a good place to start. So is just talking about same-sex marriage with your friends.

- Don't date guys who scoff at feminism. They will end up being disappointments in life, love, and bed. Trust me.

- Go see *The Vagina Monologues* on Valentine's Day (proceeds go to organizations that aim to end violence against women). Bring a date. Don't buy cheap chocolates (okay, that one is mine).

Guys

- If we don't want to have to live by sexist standards, we can't expect men to, either. The next time you find yourself judging a guy for not being "manly" enough, stop and think about what that means.

- Talk to the men in your life about feminism; let them know how sexism hurts men and women.

- If you meet a man who self-identifies as feminist, become his friend and show him off to other boys. He's a winner.

- Check out organizations like Men Can Stop Rape and the National Organization for Men Against Sexism.

Beauty

- Don't diet. Fuck them and their bullshit beauty standards. Eating can be a powerful act when the world wants you to disappear.

- Wear high heels, mascara, and whatever else you want. I sure do. But let's not forget that by doing this, we're adhering to a narrow, male-created vision of hotness. Again, this isn't to say it's wrong to want to look "hot," and to go along with the status quo from time to time, but let's not call it empowered. Call it what it is—fun and easy.

- Don't wear high heels, mascara, or whatever else *they* want. Fuck them and bullshit beauty standards.

- Call out people for using a woman's appearance to attack or judge her.

- If someone tries to use the ugly card (or the pretty one, for that matter) to silence you, keep on talking.

Politics

- Vote. Please, god, vote. Go to Women's Voices. Women Vote. (www.wvwv.org) and find out how to get involved in getting more young women interested in political participation.

- Check out the White House Project (www.thewhitehouseproject.org) and find out ways to get involved—you can take action on behalf of women candidates or find out how to become one yourself.

- Build a shrine to Ann Richards. (Okay, again, that one is mine. But feel free to steal it.)

- Run for office. Seriously, do it.

- If there's poor political representation of women in your hometown (shit, or even in your school), get working.

Spreading the Word

- Now that you know just how fantastic feminism is, go out and spread the word. Let other young women know that the "f-word" is anything but.

- If you hear someone say the dreaded phrase, "I'm not a feminist, but . . ." call them out on it. Let them know that if they have feminist opinions and values, then they're (gasp!) probably a feminist. Tell them to suck it up.

- Visit feminist blogs (cough, cough, www.feministing.com, cough). Seriously, we have an awesome list of feminist website and blogs on Feministing, so come on by.

☀ Take women's and gender studies classes and encourage others to do the same.

☀ Call yourself a feminist loud and proud. Wear a shirt. Yeah, I admit it. I love a shirt with a good message.

Yes, some of these are the easy, everyday things. There are definitely other, more involved ways to do feminism—but I'd figure it's best to start easy. Besides, everyday feminism can be the most effective (and fun). Making feminism a part of your daily life and choices really does create change all around you. But by all means, if you're loving it, go crazy and become a professional feminist.

If you've taken anything from this book, I hope at the very least you've realized all of the amazing things about feminism and what it can do for your life. That it's not an all-anti-all-the-time kind of social justice movement. It's a positive, life-changing, fun, and cool way to live your life. One that presupposes that you are worth more than your ability to please guys.

Not to get all emo at the end of the book—because that would be cliché—but the reason I wrote this book is that I believe *so* much in feminism. It changed my life for the better, and I want other young women to be able to say the same. It seems such a shame to me that so many of us shun feminism because we're afraid of the word. Because this is something that has the potential to make you think differently about everything, to make you think differently about yourself.

So, truly, thanks for reading my random feminist rants; I hope that some of it resonated with you. Young women really do have the ability to fuck shit up (in a good way), and I hope this book inspires you to start.

Five Ways You Know You're a Full Frontal Feminist

1 While you may enjoy your makeup and high heels, you realize there is something insanely fucked up about beauty standards that require women to get their vaginas trimmed. (And we're not talking hair, ladies.)

2 Fuck Ladies' Night. You'd prefer equal pay any day.

3 You realize that "slut" is just code for "I'm jealous of your sex life."

4 You want a relationship that doesn't resemble a Lifetime victim-of-the-week movie.

5 You believe you have an inalienable right to have nonprocreative sex without having to consult your pharmacist, parents, legislators, or anyone else who thinks it's their business.

Five Ways Full Frontal Feminists Are Bucking the System

1 Full frontal feminists make shopping much more enjoyable. Tired of demeaning shirts with slogans like WHO NEEDS BRAINS WHEN YOU HAVE THESE?, a group of young women called for a boycott of Abercrombie & Fitch. They were so successful in getting attention for their cause that A&F invited

them to their headquarters to help them come up with cooler sayings.

2 Full frontal feminists make sure schools are telling the truth about sex. Texas teen Shelby Knox realized that her school's sex ed program wasn't cutting it, so she took on her school board, town officials, and religious leaders to advocate for comprehensive sex ed. Her story is featured in the documentary *The Education of Shelby Knox*.

3 Full frontal feminists rock out. Young women who were done with being relegated to "video babe" status started rock camps for girls in Oregon and New York, where young girls go and learn how to play instruments, write songs, perform, and generally rock out.

4 Full frontal feminists tell the truth about what's really hot. A group of young women was sick to death of seeing all of the "hot lists" in men's magazines that judge women purely for their ability to look pouty while posing in a bikini. So they started their own—The REAL Hot 100—that showcases young women around the country for all of the amazing work they're doing in their communities.

5 Full frontal feminists make sure you can get off. In response to a sex-toy ban, young women in Memphis, Tennessee, held a "Keep Your Hands Off My Dildo" party to raise awareness about the legislation. The bill didn't stand a chance.

RESOURCES

PROVING FEMINISM IS ALIVE AND WELL

Websites

SEXUALITY AND REPRODUCTIVE RIGHTS

NARAL Pro-Choice America
www.prochoiceamerica.org

National Abortion Federation
www.prochoice.org

National Latina Institute for Reproductive Health
www.latinainstitute.org

Planned Parenthood
www.ppfa.org

Pro-Choice Public Education Project
www.protectchoice.org

Sexuality Information and Education Council of the United States
www.siecus.org

SisterSong
www.sistersong.net

VIOLENCE AGAINST WOMEN

Family Violence Prevention Fund
www.endabuse.org

Legal Momentum (women's legal rights organization)
www.legalmomentum.org

National Coalition Against Domestic Violence
www.ncadv.org

Rape, Abuse & Incest National Network
www.rainn.org

WOMEN AND THE WORKPLACE

Business & Professional Women/USA
www.bpwusa.org

Catalyst
www.catalystwomen.org

Center for Women and Work
www.cww.rutgers.edu

National Committee on Pay Equity
www.pay-equity.org

Nontraditional Employment for Women
www.new-nyc.org

FEMINIST ORGANIZATIONS AND CAMPAIGNS

Feminist Majority Foundation
www.feminist.org

National Organization for Women
www.now.org

The REAL Hot 100
www.therealhot100.org

Younger Women's Task Force
www.ywtf.org

MEN AND FEMINISM

Men Can Stop Rape
www.mencanstoprape.org

National Organization for Men Against Sexism
www.nomas.org

The White Ribbon Campaign
www.whiteribbon.ca

BODY IMAGE

About-Face
www.about-face.org

Adios, Barbie
www.adiosbarbie.com

Fat Activist Task Force
www.naafa.org/fatf

The Federal Government Source for Women's Health Information
www.4woman.gov/bodyimage

POLITICS

Center for American Women and Politics
www.cawp.rutgers.edu

Center for Women Policy Studies
www.centerwomenpolicy.org

CODEPINK
www.codepink4peace.org

EMILY's List
www.emilyslist.org

Human Rights Watch
www.hrw.org

The White House Project
www.thewhitehouseproject.org

Women's Voices. Women Vote.
www.wvwv.org

Magazines

BUST

Bitch

Colorlines

off our backs

Ms.

ROCKRGRL

Visit the Grrrl Zine Network for information on feminist zines:
www.grrrlzines.net

Books

Backlash: The Undeclared War Against American Women by Susan Faludi

The Beauty Myth: How Images of Beauty Are Used Against Women by
Naomi Wolf

BITCHfest: Ten Years of Cultural Criticism from the Pages of Bitch Magazine edited by Lisa Jervis and Andi Zeisler

Body Outlaws: Rewriting the Rules of Beauty and Body Image edited by Ophira Edut

The Body Project: An Intimate History of American Girls by Joan Jacobs Brumberg

The Boundaries of Her Body: The Troubling History of Women's Rights in America by Debran Rowland

The Bust Guide to the New Girl Order edited by Marcelle Karp and Debbie Stoller

Colonize This! Young Women of Color on Today's Feminism edited by Daisy Hernández and Bushra Rehman

Cunt: A Declaration of Independence by Inga Muscio

Dilemmas of Desire: Teenage Girls Talk about Sexuality by Deborah L. Tolman

FAT!SO? Because You Don't Have to Apologize for your Size! by Marilyn Wann

Female Chauvinist Pigs: Women and the Rise of Raunch Culture by Ariel Levy

Feminism Is for Everybody: Passionate Politics by bell hooks

The Fire This Time: Young Activists and the New Feminism edited by Vivien Labaton and Dawn Lundy Martin

The F-Word: Feminism in Jeopardy by Kristin Rowe-Finkbeiner

A Girl's Guide to Taking over the World: Writings from the Girl Zine Revolution by Tristan Taormino

Kiss My Tiara: How to Rule the World as a Smartmouth Goddess by Susan Jane Gilman

Listen Up: Voices from the Next Feminist Generation edited by Barbara Findlen

Manifesta: Young Women, Feminism, and the Future by Jennifer Baumgardner

Ophelia Speaks: Adolescent Girls Write About Their Search for Self edited by Sara Shandler

Our Bodies, Ourselves by the Boston Women's Health Book Collective

Slut! Growing Up Female with a Bad Reputation by Leora Tanenbaum

Sugar in the Raw: Voices of Young Black Girls in America by Rebecca Carroll

Third Wave Agenda: Being Feminist, Doing Feminism edited by Leslie Heywood and Jennifer Drake

To Be Real: Telling the Truth and Changing the Face of Feminism edited by Rebecca Walker

We Don't Need Another Wave: Dispatches from the Next Generation of Feminists edited by Melody Berger

Woman: An Intimate Geography, by Natalie Angier

Yell-Oh Girls!: Emerging Voices Explore Culture, Identity, and Growing Up Asian American edited by Vickie Nam

Hotlines

National Domestic Violence Hotline: (800) 799-SAFE (799-7233)

National Hopeline Network: (800) SUICIDE (784-2433)

National STD/HIV Hotline: (800) 227-8922

Rape, Abuse & Incest National Network: (800) 656-HOPE (656-4673)

Youth Crisis Hotline: (800) HIT-HOME (448-4663)

NOTES

1 You're a Hardcore Feminist. I Swear.

1 Ginia Bellafante. "Is Feminism Dead?" *Time* magazine, June 29, 1998.

2 Lawrence Summers is the former president of Harvard University. At a conference about women and minorities in science and engineering while he was still president, Summers theorized that one of the reasons for the lower number of women in the math and science fields was that women don't have the same "natural" or "innate" ability as men.

3 Christine John, a first-year teacher at the Village Adventist Elementary School in Berrien Springs, Michigan, was placed on administrative leave for getting pregnant out of wedlock in 2005. Also in 2005, Michelle McCusker, an unmarried teacher at St. Rose of Lima School in Queens, New York, was fired after she told school officials she was pregnant.

4 Monique Stuart. "Slutty Feminism," *The Washington Times,* January 1, 2006.

5 I'll provide the following articles just to give you a sampling of what's out there:

Phyllis Schlafly. "Feminist Dream Becomes Nightmare," Human Events Online, May 18, 2004; Carey Roberts. "Amnesty Stuck on the Shoals of Political Correctness," MensNewsDaily.com, June 4, 2005; David

Usher. "Feminism, the WKKK, and the Gender-Lynching of Michael Jackson," MensNewsDaily.com, April 21, 2005.

6 Mary Rettig. "CWA Official: Rising Crime Among Women Linked to Feminist Agenda," AgapePress, October 27, 2005.

7 Ibid.

8 Vaginal "rejuvenation" is the newest form of plastic surgery by which women can get labiaplasties, vaginal tightening, and liposuction on their labia.

9 *The American Heritage Dictionary.*

10 Rebecca Traister. "The F-Word," Salon.com, July 5, 2005.

11 Ibid.

12 Post in response to Rebecca Traister's "The F-Word." Found online at: www.sabreean.com/?p=10.

2 Feminists Do It Better (and Other Sex Tips)

1 Sexuality Information and Education Council of the United States.

2 Representative Henry Waxman. "The Content of Federally Funded Abstinence-Only Education Programs," U.S. House of Representatives Committee on Government Reform, December 2004.

3 Gail Schontzler. "Abstinence speaker pushed religion in school, dad charges," *The Daily Chronicle*, May 11, 2005.

4 Representative Henry Waxman.

5 Ibid.

6 Ibid.

7 "In Their Own Words: What Abstinence-Only-Until-Marriage Programs Say," Sexuality Information and Education Council of the United States, August 2005.

8 Quoted in Camille Hahn. "Virgin Territory," *Ms.* magazine, fall 2004.

9 "Jessica Simpson's Virgin Vow," *Female First,* December 30, 2004. Found online at: www.femalefirst.co.uk/entertainment.

10 Reginald Finger. "Association of Virginity at Age 18 with Educational, Economic, Social, and Health Outcomes in Middle Adulthood," *Adolescent & Family Health,* April 2004.

11 Reports of Child Abuse and Neglect (HB 580).

12 Jodi Wilgoren. "In Nebraska, Rape Charge Follows Legal Marriage, in Kansas, to 14-Year-Old," *The New York Times,* August 20, 2005.

13 Jonathan Amos. "Ancient phallus unearthed in cave," BBC News, July 25, 2005.

14 From a December 1994 speech at a United Nations–sponsored conference on AIDS. Found online at: www.rotten.com/library/sex/masturbation.

15 "Texas mom faces trial for selling sex toys," Reuters, February 11, 2004.

16 Michael Lemonicka. "Teen Twist on Sex," *Time* magazine, September 19, 2005.

3 Pop Culture Gone Wild

1 This term was coined by Pamela Paul in her new book by the same name. Pamela Paul. *Pornified: How Pornography Is Transforming Our Lives, Our Relationships, and Our Families* (New York: Henry Holt, 2005).

2 Ariel Levy. *Female Chauvinist Pigs: Women and the Rise of Raunch Culture* (New York: Free Press, 2006).

3 Jennifer Baumgardner. "Feminism Is a Failure, and Other Myths," AlterNet, November 17, 2005.

4 Whitney Joiner. "Live girl-on-girl action!" Salon.com, June 20, 2006.

5 From a Feministing interview with Rachel Kramer Bussel.

6 R. Scott Moxley. "Slammer Time," *OC Weekly*, October 7, 2005.

7 Erin Woods. "Sex and intoxication among women more common on spring break, according to AMA poll," AMA press release, March 8, 2006.

8 Audio interview with Janice Crouse, senior fellow with the Beverly LaHaye Institute, Concerned Women for America. Found online at: www.cwfa.org/articles.

4 The Blame (and Shame) Game

1 National Crime Victimization Survey, Bureau of Justice Statistics' Crime and Victims Statistics, 2004. Found online at: www.rainn.org/statistics.

2 "Women in jeans 'cannot be raped'," BBC News, February 11, 1999. Found online at: www.news.bbc.co.uk/1/hi/world.

3 Naomi Schaefer Riley. "Ladies, You Should Know Better: How feminism wages war on common sense," *The Wall Street Journal,* April 14, 2006.

4 Found online at: www.cnn.com/2006/WORLD/europe.

5 Sexual assault research, Amnesty International, November 2005. Found online at: www.amnesty.org.uk/news.

6 R. Scott Moxley. "Slammer Time," *OC Weekly,* October 27, 2005. Found online at: www.ocweekly.com/news.

7 R. Scott Moxley. "Hung Jury?" *OC Weekly,* June 24, 2004. Found online at: www.ocweekly.com/news.

8 "Three Men Receive Six-Year Sentences in Sexual Assault Case," NBC News, March 10, 2006. Found online at: www.nbc4.tv/news.

9 "Anti-rape device postponed," SABC News, June 21, 2006. Found online at: www.sabcnews.com/south_africa.

10 Andrea Medea and Kathleen Thompson. "The Little Rapes, Sexual Harassment: The Link Joining Gender Stratification, Sexuality, and Women's Economic Status" (New York: Farrar, Straus and Giroux, 1974).

11 Holla Back NYC. Found online at: www.hollabacknyc.blogspot.com.

5 If These Uterine Walls Could Talk

1 "UW Birth Control Help 'Outrages' Rep," *The Capitol Times,* March 1, 2005.

2 "Pharmacist cites sin in birth control case," Associated Press. Found online at: www.washtimes.com/national.

3 Dan Gransinger. "Absolving pharmacist's conscience," letter to the editor, *The Arizona Republic,* April 15, 2005. Found online at: www.azcentral.com/arizonarepublic/opinions.

4 Russell Shorto. "Contra-Contraception," *The New York Times Magazine,* May 7, 2006.

5 "Why do women have abortions?" Guttmacher Institute press release, September 6, 2005. Found online at: www.guttmacher.org/media.

6 "South Dakota Abortion Ban," PBS Online News Hour. Found online at: www.pbs.org/newshour.

7 Bob Johnson. "Proposals would ban abortions," Associated Press, October 21, 2006. Found online at: www.montgomeryadvertiser.com/apps/pbcs.dll/article.

8 Ellie Lee. "The Context for the Development of 'Post-Abortion Syndrome.'" The Prochoice Forum. Found online at: www.prochoiceforum.org.uk/

9 Amanda Marcotte. "Exposing Anti-Choice Abortion Clinics," Alternet, May 1, 2006.

10 Rebecca Walsh. "Senate: Incestuous dad knows best," *The Salt Lake Tribune,* February 28, 2006.

11 HB 187: Unmarried women; prohibition on provision of certain intervening medical technology.

12 Katherine Gillespie. "Defining Reproductive Freedom for Women 'Living Under a Microscope': Relf v. Weinberger and the Involuntary Sterilization of Poor Women of Color," 2000. Found online at: www.law.georgetown.edu/glh/gillespie.

13 Betsy Hartmann. "Cracking Open Crack," Znet, October 22, 1999. Found online at: www.zmag.org/ZSustainers/ZDaily.

14 From a conversation with Wyndi Anderson, March 7, 2006.

6 Material World

1 "Kerry's 'Fresh Start' Is A False Start, IWF Decries Use of Misleading Statistics on Wage Gap," press release, October 22, 2004. Found online at: www.iwf.org/issues.

2 "Senate amendment would reinstate data collection for women at the Bureau of Labor Statistics," October 27, 2005. Found online at: www.now.org/issues/economic.

3 Shankar Vedantam. "Women in Top Ranks Pull Up the Pay of Others," *The Washington Post,* August 13, 2006.

4 Citizens for Responsibility and Ethics in Washington (CREW). Found online at: www.citizensforethics.org/activities.

5 "'Older' women win Virgin discrimination case," ABC News, October 10, 2005. Found online at: www.abc.net.au/news.

6 Found online at: www.breaktheglassceiling.com/statistics-women.

7 "WORKPLACE BIAS?" PBS, Online News Hour, July 5, 2004. Found online at: www.pbs.org/newshour.

8 Equal Employment Opportunity Commission. Found online at: www.eeoc.gov/types/sexual_harassment.

9 CNN. Found online at: www.cnn.com/2006/LAW.

10 "Sexual Abuse by Military Recruiters, More Than 100 Women Raped Or Assaulted By Recruiters In Past Year," August 20, 2006. Found online at: www.cbsnews.com/stories.

11 Feministing interview. Found online at: www.feministing.com/archives.

12 Ibid.

13 Lisa Belkin. "The Opt-Out Revolution," *The New York Times Magazine,* October 26, 2003.

14 The Center for Economic Policy and Research. "Are Women Opting Out?" Found online at www.cepr.net/publications.

15 Ibid.

16 Louis Uchitelle and David Leonhardt. "Men Not Working, and Not Wanting Just Any Job," *The New York Times,* July 31, 2006.

17 "U.S. mothers deserve $134,121 in salary," Reuters Study, May 3, 2006.

18 Linda Hirshman. *Get to Work: A Manifesto for Women of the World* (New York: Viking Adult, 2006).

19 Mindy Farabee. "Linda Hirshman's Manifesto for Women," *LA CityBeat,* September 5, 2006.

20 The Family Initiative, Legal Momentum. Research done by the project found that some Americans are allocating as much as 50 percent of their salaries to childcare expenses.

21 Legal Momentum. Found online at: www.legalmomentum.org/legalmomentum/programs/familyinitiative.

22 Ibid.

23 "Congressional Child Care," *The Washington Post,* Tuesday, May 16, 2006.

24 Wade Horn. "Wedded to Marriage," National Review Online, August 9, 2005. Found online at: www.nationalreview.com/comment.

25 Legal Momentum. Found online at: www.legalmomentum.org/legalmomentum/inthecourts.

26 Marriage Savers Program. Found online at: www.marriagesavers.org.

27 Legal Momentum. Found online at: www.legalmomentum.org/legalmomentum/programs/equalityworks.

28 Michael Noer. "Don't Marry Career Women," *Forbes,* August 22, 2006.

7 My Big Fat Unnecessary Wedding and Other Dating Diseases

1 "Same-Sex Marriage: The Fight for Equality Gains Momentum," NOW. Found online at: www.now.org/nnt.

2 "Marriage Protection Week, 2003, A Proclamation." Found online at: www.whitehouse.gov/news/releases.

8 "Real" Women Have Babies

1 Kathryn Joyce. "Arrows for the War," *The Nation.* November 27, 2006.

2 Report of the South Dakota Task Force to Study Abortion. Available online at: www.feministing.com/SD_abortion_taskforce_report.pdf.

3 January Payne. "Forever Pregnant," *The Washington Post,* May 16, 2006.

4 Lynn Paltrow. "Punishment For Pregnant Women," *Alternet* July 18, 2006.

5 Katha Pollitt. "Pregnant and Dangerous," *The Nation,* April 8, 2004.

6 Found online at: www.advocatesforpregnantwomen.org/issues/in_the_states/.

7 Rick Montgomery. "New Wave of 'Fetal Protectionism' Decried," *Lexington Herald-Leader,* July 10, 2006.

8 Lynn Paltrow. "Punishment For Pregnant Women," *Alternet,* July 18, 2006.

9 From an email exchange with Wyndi Anderson of National Advocates for Pregnant Women.

10 Mike Stobbe. "C-Sections in U.S. Are at All-Time High," *The Associated Press,* November 15, 2005.

11 Joan Ryan. "Balancing the risks in a healthy delivery," International Awareness Caesarean Netowrk, Inc., Press Kit. November 9, 2003.

12 Anemona Hartocollis. "Home Delivery is Available," *The New York Times,* June 2, 2005.

13 The Associated Press. "New Alabama law allows breast-feeding in public," July 5, 2006.

14 The Associated Press. "30 Protest Ejection of Nursing Passenger," ABC News, November 15, 2006.

15 Kansas Department of Health and Environment, KDHE reminds public about health benefits of breastfeeding and mother's rights, during World Breastfeeding Week, August 2, 2006.

16 Feministing interview with Kristin Rowe-Finkbeiner, September 09, 2006. Available online at http://feministing.com/archives/.

17 Sharon Jayson. "Women like being mothers but say they get no respect," *USA Today,* May 1, 2005.

18 Found online at: http://www.momsrising.org/aboutmomsrising.

9 I Promise I Won't Say "Herstory"

1 Found online at: www.reference.com/browse/wiki/Elizabeth_Cady_Stanton.

2 Sojourner Truth. "Ain't I a Woman?" Women's Convention, Ohio, 1851.

3 Betty Friedan. *The Feminine Mystique* (New York: Dell Publishing Co., 1963).

4 National Organization for Women's Statement of Purpose, 1966.

5 "Feminist Majority Foundation, *Ms.* Magazine, and Feminist Majority Foundation Join Forces," November 12, 2001. Found online at: www.feminist.org/news.

6 *Roe v. Wade,* 410 U.S. 113, No. 70–18, January 22, 1973. Found online at: www.law.cornell.edu/supct/html/histories.

7 The Civil Rights Act of 1964, 88th Congress, H. R. 7152, July 2, 1964.

8 Angela Davis is a civil rights activist and feminist; my favorite book by her is *Women, Race and Class* (London: The Women's Press Ltd., 1981).

9 Susan Brownmiller. *Against Our Will: Men, Women and Rape* (New York: Simon & Schuster, 1975).

10 Alice Walker, author of *The Color Purple*, coined the word "womanist."

11 Lesbian theory started to pop up in the '60s alongside feminism.

12 "Sex wars" refers to debates within the second-wave feminist community surrounding issues of sexuality, especially pornography.

13 Feministe. Found online at: www.feministe.us/blog/archives.

14 Susan Faludi. *Backlash: The Undeclared War Against American Women* (New York: Anchor Books, 1992).

15 Joanne Smith talked to me about her experience at the NOW conference when I was writing an article on the event for *The Guardian*.

10 Boys Do Cry

1 Lakshmi Chaudhry. "Men Growing Up to Be Boys," *In These Times,* March 17, 2006.

2 Rebecca Traister. "Attack of the Listless Lads," Salon.com, September 20, 2005.

3 Interview with Michael Kimmel, PhD, PBS. Found online at: www.pbs.org/kued/nosafeplace.

4 Ibid.

5 Found online at www.participate.net.

6 "Seven Principles for Bringing Up Boys." Found online at: www.focusonyourchild.com/develop.

7 "Countering Radical Feminism's Agenda." Found online at: www.focusonyourchild.com.

8 Huibin Amee Chew. "Why The War Is Sexist," Znet, December 1, 2005. Found online at: www.zmag.org/content.

9 Cynthia Enloe. *Maneuvers: The International Politics of Militarizing Women's Lives* (Berkeley, CA: University of California Press, 2000).

10 Amnesty International, "Lives blown apart: Crimes against women in times of conflict," December 2004. Found online at: http://web.amnesty.org/library.

11 Robert Jensen. "The High Cost of Manliness," Alternet, September 8, 2006.

11 Beauty Cult

1 Althouse is run by University of Wisconsin law professor Ann Althouse. Found online at: www.althouse.blogspot.com.

2 "Women Now Have Equal Sexuality Rights," press release, Laser Vaginal Rejuvenation Institute of New York. Found online at: www.prweb.com/releases.

3 "New Message to Models: Eat!" ABC News, September 15, 2006. Found online at: www.abcnews.go.com/Entertainment.

4 "Skinny models banned from catwalk," CNN, September 13, 2006. Found online at: www.cnn.com/2006/WORLD/europe.

5 "Gaultier swaps Size 0 models for 'Size 20,'" the *Daily Mail,* October 4, 2006. Found online at: www.dailymail.co.uk/pages.

12 *Sex and the City* Voters, My Ass

1 Women Officeholders 2006, Center for American Women and Politics, Rutgers University.

2 University at Albany, State University of New York, Women in State Policy Leadership, 1998–2005. *An Analysis of Slow and Uneven Progress, A Report of the Center for Women in Government & Civil Society.* Winter 2006.

3 Women's Voices. Women Vote. Found online at: www.wvwv.org.

4 Steve Vogel. "Owens Assails Schaefer's Remarks." *The Washington Post,* September 6, 2006.

5 Phyllis Jordan. "Schaefer Remarks Criticized, Maryland Moment," *The Washington Post,* February 15, 2006. Found online at: http://blog.washingtonpost.com/annapolis.

6 "Executive Summary, Framing Gender on the Campaign Trail, Style Over Substance: Spotlight on Elizabeth Dole." Found online at: www.thewhitehouseproject.org/v2/researchandreports.

7   Loretta Nall campaign blog. Found online at:
    www.nallforgovernor.blogspot.com.

8   John Podhoretz on Hillary Clinton's "virtues," Media Matters,
    May 10, 2006. Found online at: www.mediamatters.org/items.

9   Ibid.

10 Robin Toner. "Women Wage Key Campaigns for Democrats," *The New
    York Times,* March 24, 2006.

11 Ann Friedman, March 24, 2006. Found online at:
    www.feministing.com/archives.

12 Josh Gerstain. "Maloney Wins Support of ACLU For Regulation of
    Abortion Ads," *The New York Sun,* March 31, 2006.

13 Jeremy Peters. "F.D.A. Plans to Consider Morning-After Pill,"
    The New York Times, July 31, 2006.

14 "Kansas Anti-Abortion Bill Veto Sticks," Associated Press, Thursday,
    April 28, 2005.

15 Found online at: www.house.gov/waters.

16 R. G. Ratcliffe and Anne Marie Kilday. "Groundbreaking politician, quint-
    essential Texas woman," *The Houston Chronicle,* September 14, 2006.

17 Bella Abzug was an outspoken congresswoman who fought tirelessly
    for women's rights. She died in 1998. Read more about her online at:
    www.womenshistory.about.com/cs/quotes.

18 Patricia Schroeder was Colorado's first woman in Congress. Read more
    about her online at: www.womenshistory.about.com/cs/quotes.

19 John Kerry campaign button.

20 "Marriage Gap Bigger Than Gender Gap, With Married People More
    Supportive Than Singles Are To Bush and Republicans, Annenberg Data
    Show," National Annenberg Election Survey, July 2, 2004.

21 Quoted in Ruth Rosen. "Women Really on Their Own," *The Nation,*
    October 29, 2004.

22 The 50/50 Campaign, Women's Environment & Development Organization. Found online at: www.wedo.org/programs.

23 Found online at: wedo.org/campaigns.aspx?mode=5050main.

24 Getting the Balance Right in National Parliaments, 50/50 Campaign, Women's Environment & Development Organization.

25 Found online at: www.state.gov/g/drl/rls/hrrpt.

26 Found online at: www.sweden.se/templates.

13 A Quick Academic Aside

1 Lorde, Audre. "Age, Race, Class and Sex," *Race, Class and Gender in the United States*, Fourth Edition. Ed. By Paula S. Rothenberg, St. Martin's Press, 1998.

2 Working Group on Women and Human Rights, Center for Women's Global Leadership, Rugters University. Found online at: www.cwgl.rutgers.edu/globalcenter/policy/bkgdbrfintersec.html.

3 McIntosh, Peggy. *White Privilege: Unpacking the Invisible Knapsack*, Found online at: http://seamonkey.ed.asu.edu/ ~ mcisaac/emc598ge/Unpacking.html.

4 Lorde, Audre. "Age, Race, Class and Sex," *Race, Class and Gender in the United States,* Fourth Edition. Ed. By Paula S. Rothenberg, St. Martin's Press, 1998.

5 Pharr, Suzanne. "Homophobia as a Weapon of Sexism," *Class and Gender in the United States*, Fourth Edition. Ed. By Paula S. Rothenberg, St. Martin's Press, 1998.

6 Ibid.

14 Get to It

1 Holla Back. Found online at: www.hollabacknyc.blogspot.com.

ACKNOWLEDGMENTS

I'd like to give tremendous thanks to everyone who helped and supported me as I was writing this book: my editor Brooke Warner, my agent Tracy Brown, my ever-patient parents Nancy and Phil Valenti, Vanessa Valenti, Gwen Beetham, Raymond Clepper, Celina De Leon, Evan Derkacz, Ann Friedman, Allison Heiny, Adam Joseph, Amanda Marcotte, Christine Marron, Maureen McFadden, Kate Mogulescu, Jen Moseley, Samhita Mukhopadhyay, Joan Ross-Frankson, Bill Scher, Rebecca Traister, all the feminist bloggers out there who inspire me, and—with never-ending appreciation—all of the readers and supporters of Feministing.com.

ABOUT THE AUTHOR

Jessica Valenti—called one of the Top 100 Inspiring Women in the world by *The Guardian*—is the author of four books on feminism, politics, and culture. Jessica is also the founder of Feministing.com, which *Columbia Journalism Review* called "head and shoulders above almost any writing on women's issues in mainstream media." Her writing has appeared in *The Washington Post, The Nation, The Guardian (UK), The American Prospect, Ms.* magazine, *Salon,* and *Bitch* magazine.

She received her Masters degree in Women's and Gender Studies from Rutgers University.

Jessica lives with her husband and daughter in New York.

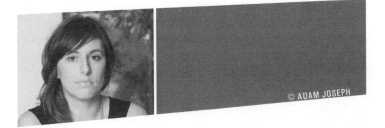

© ADAM JOSEPH

SELECTED TITLES FROM SEAL PRESS

A Little F'd Up: Why Feminism Is Not a Dirty Word, by Julie Zeilinger. $16.00, 978-1-58005-371-6. A wry, witty overview of feminism's past and present from the creator of *FBomb,* the popular feminist blog for young people.

F 'em!: Goo Goo, Gaga, and Some Thoughts on Balls, by Jennifer Baumgardner. $17.00, 978-1-58005-360-0. A collection of essays—plus interviews with well-known feminists—by *Manifesta* co-author Jennifer Baumgardner on everything from purity balls to Lady Gaga.

What You Really Really Want: The Smart Girl's Shame-Free Guide to Sex and Safety, by Jaclyn Friedman. $17.00, 978-1-58005-344-0. An educational and interactive guide that gives young women the tools they need to decipher the modern world's confusing, hypersexualized landscape and define their own sexual identity.

Get Opinionated: A Progressive's Guide to Finding Your Voice (and Taking A Little Action), by Amanda Marcotte. $15.95, 978-1-58005-302-0. Hilarious, bold, and very opinionated, this book helps young women get a handle on the issues they care about—and provides suggestions for the small steps they can take towards change.

Yes Means Yes: Visions of Female Sexual Power and A World Without Rape, by Jaclyn Friedman and Jessica Valenti. $16.95, 978-1-58005-257-3. This powerful and revolutionary anthology offers a paradigm shift from the "No Means No" model, challenging men and women to truly value female sexuality and ultimately end rape.

The Guy's Guide to Feminism, by Michael Kaufman & Michael Kimmel. $16.00, 978-1-58005-362-4. A hip and accessible guide that illustrates how understanding and supporting feminism can help men live richer, fuller, and happier lives.

Find Seal Press Online
www.SealPress.com
www.Facebook.com/SealPress
Twitter: @SealPress

32953012543916